Fast Over 40

CM Monteleone

Cover image: J. Anthony Martinez

Back cover image: Margaret Monteleone

Cover and interior design: Alison Harney

Illustrations: Cynthia Monteleone

The information included in this book is for educational and entertainment purposes only. It is not intended or implied to be a substitute for professional medical advice. The reader should always consult with his or her healthcare provider before starting or changing nutrition or exercise routines. The statements in this book have not been evaluated by the Food and Drug Administration. The products or supplements in this book are not intended to diagnose, treat, cure or prevent any disease. The authors, contributors and publisher expressly disclaim responsibility for any adverse effects that may result from the use or application of the information contained in this book. The opinions and views of the author are not necessarily the opinion of the workout contributors.

For Charles, the legend lives on...

Table of Contents

Introduction

Our bodies are absolutely amazing pieces of machinery. I'm not sure why we forget to appreciate all of the completely intricate workings of our electrical system, but we do. Let's face it, we absolutely take it for granted! We forget and dismiss the complex and little understood tissues, bones, and blood…. Like a dried dandelion in the wind, we blow it away, wishing for better health, while ignoring the knowledge to get there. Most of our lives we assume our body is less than what it is worth—that is…our LIFE.

At what point does someone teach us that it is ok to abuse our body with a steady stream of modern toxins? When do we learn that is fine for our health to sit all day at a computer, go home, sit all night in front of a TV and then lay restless in bed, only to go and do it all over again, feverishly attempting to cover our weariness with temporary band-aids like alcohol and sugar?

Why did we learn that we are merely human and not superheroes?

I hope to change that, maybe even just a little bit, by sharing my experience. You see, I believe anyone can bring out their inner superhero. I believe you can do this!

Me on Maui, at the time of writing, age 44.
Photo: Margaret Monteleone

PART ONE:
The Stories

Welo kihei a ke A'eola

Translation: The shoulder covering fluttered in the A'eola wind.
Traveled with speed. The runner went so fast that his kihei (cape) stood
straight out behind as he ran against the A'eola wind.[1]

Background

I am a guest in the place that I live. That is to say: I am not from here but
temporarily inhabiting the geographical location in which I spend my
days until I perish from this life. I am a guest of my island. It is a blessing
to be able to breathe tropical air daily; to feel a warm trade wind breezing
through my hair. I am fortunate to look across the horizon to the vast
azure ocean or behind me to the commanding verdant mountains.

In a way, we are all guests of our location. We can focus on acquiring
possessions, however, but ultimately, we are temporary while the place is
continuous. During this temporary state, we have the ability to become
the individual we want to become. We have, in our possession, this very
moment, the building blocks to take our bodies and make them stronger
than we ever thought, through a manipulation of our gene expression. We
are born with what our parents gave us, sure, but we can shape ourselves
and how our cells react, through environment and decisions. Simple
formulas of food choice and exercise, take us on a path to become what we
want to become. Anyone and everyone can make better choices!

I am a guest of the island of Maui, Hawaii. According to my DNA report,
I am only 2 percent East Asian. According to my family history (and
DNA) I am mostly Navajo, Apache, and German. All three of which have

tremendous histories of incorporating running into their cultures. The Navajo believe in rising and facing the sun every morning for a run. The Apache tribes are well noted in history to have used running to build great warriors. Ancient Germanic tribes, just like other ancient cultures, trained their male children early on to be fast and strong for battle.

I live and raise my family in Hawaii, however, and I am inspired by the rich stories of the people who came before me. On these islands, settled by Polynesian tribes long ago, the atmosphere brings a saturation of magic and history in every turn. It is no wonder that millions flock to this paradise every year. In my opinion, it is more than just the pleasant weather and beautiful flowering trees that bring a smile. It is the strong sense of ancient wisdom combined with respect for nature that gives Maui the quiet sense of the supernatural. I often hear people say things like: "Maui is a healing place." I have also seen firsthand those who disrespect the island get booted off rather quickly by unlucky turns of events or the unidentifiable "island fever."

When I am here, I am home. I have never felt more at home in my life. When I leave, I feel a piece of me gone. This is how I "feel" Maui. I make sure to bring with me a flower to wear in my hair when I compete in my races, so that I have a piece of my island with me, a piece of inspiration from the place of my temporary habitation, a piece of my family and the community that supports me.

In Ancient Hawaii, there exists a great tradition of athleticism and that certainly included running. During the time period when noble families with kings or chiefs (called Ali'i– ah lee ee) ruled the islands, a type of runner emerged to assist the kings. They were called kukini (koo-kee-nee). The kukini literally "ran" errands. Whatever the king desired, it was the kukini's honor to run, obtain and return. They were also messengers, travelling across the lands to villages to quickly deliver information. They were placed high in society and were so revered they were not to be spoken to while on a king's mission. With these extreme running skills, they became a type of superhero of their day. The legends grew of how fast and how far the kukini could go. In one tale, a kukini on Maui could run around the whole island in a day! In these modern times, it is difficult to get around in a car in 24 hours.

The kukini became as popular as professional athletes today. At the annual harvest celebration, during the athletic competition known as the Makahiki games, the runners were pitted against each other in sprints and bets were made. In order to prepare for these "errands" and races, the kukini recognized the importance of nutrition, training and community. They ate a restricted diet, performed sprint drills like walking on their toes for extended periods of time, and honored their kingdom with their work. They are a great, inspirational example of changing your mind, body, and spirit to achieve seemingly impossible feats.

Also in ancient times, the warriors were known for their Olakino Maika'i (Oh-la-kee-no Mai-ka-ee) or their great physical health that came from honoring their bodies with healthy food and vigorous exercise. It is this type of inspiration, magic, and harmony that I hope to share with you in this book.

I was not always a number one runner in the world. At one point, not too long ago, I was just starting out like you may be. I was 20 pounds heavier, definitely not so strong, and carrying leftover baby weight from my third child. One day, my daughter, who was 11 at the time, asked me if I could train her in the 400 meters so that she could run track in college "like mom did." Delighted, I agreed and up to the local high school track we went!

We ran one lap around the track as fast as we could. Collapsing with exhaustion and weakness at the finish line with an unimpressive pace of about one minute and 30 seconds, I had just run the hardest 400 meters of my life. The important thing to note about this day was not my time. I had done zero running in the past 20 years! The exciting part was that I started. I kept showing up week after week. I was consistent in my dedication.

After a year, I entered a national competition for the 400 meters and received a 4th place ribbon. Now, of course I was pleased to win an award, but a ribbon! Ugh! I was so close to a medal. One tenth of a second to be exact. I became hungry to see how far I could go, hungry for medals and

The beginning of my sprint journey (left) and 3 years later (right).
Photo by J. Anthony Martinez

a national championship. I wanted to see just how well I could optimize my human self and become a warrior like the ancestors of my past and the Ancient Hawaiians that inhabited this place before me. I wanted to be the best in the nation. I would settle for no less.

I dedicated myself to learning the tricks and biohacks to optimizing myself. I learned how to reverse the natural pitfalls of aging. Instead of falling into the cold, dark well of impending aging related injuries and health issues, I learned to do my own research. I learned to fuel for optimal athletic performance, prevent injury, and become strong and FAST OVER 40. In fact, I have never missed a competition due to injury because I learned how to eat and train to optimize my tendons and tissues. I continued on my journey to become a certified Metabolic Analytics Practitioner. I studied directly under the founder of the program, the legendary Charles Poliquin.

I am now grateful to be able to help and advise multitudes of athletes ranging from middle-aged women wishing for more energy and increased fitness to Olympic and professional athletes in an array of sports. Often, my local physician sends his patients my way when their blood work looks ok but their symptoms do not subside with conventional Western medical treatment. He says he deals in black and white, and to wade through the gray to find the answer: "Go to Cynthia." I meet with clients either over the phone or in person and make an initial assessment based on our interview. After that, if in person, I measure where they store their body fat. Where you store body fat varies from person to person, and the locations the body selects indicates probable health issues according to Chinese medicine. For instance: those storing fat in their hamstrings tend to have problems with managing environmental toxins that mimic estrogens. By measuring 14 different places, I can tell from the ratio of those measurements how to proceed to help balance the individual's system through diet, supplements, rest, and exercise. If unable to measure, I give a general consultation based on symptoms and history, while also working with the client's physician to help each person reach their goal. This book is a more generalized approach to helping you achieve your goals, offering methods that have worked well for a large percentage of my clientele. After reading it, if you would like a personalized

Winning the W40 400m National Championship 2019,
Photo: Sandy Lee Triolo

approach, please feel welcome to schedule a consultation via the website MAM808.com.

After learning the "secret intelligence" of how to metabolically thrive, I won the gold medal in the Indoor and Outdoor National Championships in 4 events the following year. After that, I kept going, and became the best in the World, a World Champion, running my gold medal winning race in a FASTER time than I ran 22 years prior in college! How was this possible?

It is my passion to share the gift of my inspiration and experiences with you! I encourage you to start where you are and become your optimized superhuman, superhero self.

Becoming a World Champion, 2019.
Photo: Margaret Monteleone

Section I.
Brain Stimulation/Mind
Developing Superhero Mentality with Food

"E hinu auane'i na nuku he pomaika'i ko laila"
"Where the mouths are shiny with fat food, prosperity is there"[2]

The Superhero Makoa

Once upon a time several hundred years ago there was a Hawaiian King named Kamehameha the Great. The King, like most Hawaiian royalty, was a great warrior, committed athlete, and tall, but Kamehameha was larger than most—he was seven feet tall and 300 pounds.

As you might imagine, he was frequently hungry.

One morning while sipping his 'awa and looking out over the silvery ocean he decided he needed his favorite type of fish to accompany the bitter, nootropic drink derived from kava root. He called upon his best runner Makoa.

Makoa was no dwarf himself. He had semi-circle tattoos adorning his eyes and two goat tattoos above his brow. He appeared before the king, tugging at this long beard knotted twice at the top, before flaring out, so as to resemble a tassel.[3]

"Makoa, bring me some mullet from the pond of Waiakea to eat with my 'awa," the King requested. The journey, 80 miles there and back, took a normal man four days to travel as the land was full of ravines, rocky gulches, and rugged trails. Furthermore, the owner of the fish pond was an enemy of the King's, Keawemauhili, who had been threatening to start up trouble again.

Off went Makoa, his long, curly black hair shaved along the sides, bundled up at the top in a neat knot. Makoa, long acquainted with the king, understood he was to find more than fish.

Makoa returned the "sun still high," and the fish still wriggling with life. In addition to the largest fish carefully wrapped in seaweed, Makoa carried

Illustration by CM Monteleone

another precious bundle. Enclosed in a sacred Hawaiian ti leaf were two white rocks—a symbol to the king of peace and good will. War would not be waged between these two, at this time.

The King was pleased and invited Makoa to share his meal.

In local tradition, if one was a fast runner, they were called the "brother of Makoa." These elite high class of men were often given high protein foods like poultry to eat, whereas the commoners and most women were not allowed to eat these and certain other foods. By breeding amongst the elite class, with protein rich diets in meat and fish, the royal Hawaiians, not the commoners, maintained extremely athletic physiques as was so noted by the Europeans' first impressions. How big were they? Upon excavating to build a local hotel, a 3-foot shin bone was found! The father of Kamehameha was said to be possibly 10 or 11 feet tall according to his measurements recorded on the sacred stone of his namesake—the Keoua stone on the island of Hawai'i.

Already the description of Makoa, like the description of so many of the kukini and warriors, paints a vivid description of a superhero! Don't we all want to be the brother/sister of Makoa? To become a legend in our own time for being our optimal superhuman self? To not only run your fastest, but also deliver sustenance and peace? But where to begin? What to do first?

Start Where You Are

"I'm just not motivated to exercise," says Kendall, a great example of metabolic clientele I will be sharing with you. Kendall, a pretty girl in her early 30's with long brunette hair tied neatly back tells me, "I used to love to be active, but now I have no energy." My quick personality assessment based on visual cues, tells me that she is smart, professional, organized and…well, tired. Her outfit is tidy and classy but her skin is pale: like gray clouds on an overcast day. Her demeanor is intelligent and charming but her eyes have lost their sparkle.

I have seen this before, in clients. But even more importantly, I have BEEN this before, myself. I can relate. As I listen to her talk, I think of a time in my late 20's when my good friend, reminiscent of the no nonsense character Miranda from *Sex in the City,* looked at me from across the table and very bluntly stated, "What happened to you?" I had at one point, too, become lifeless, unmotivated, and gray. I knew I didn't feel right. I knew something was off. But what?

A few years later someone gave me the answer. Neurotransmitters! What was I doing to spark my neurotransmitters to give me energy, motivation… life? It turns out that the food we eat and the nutrition we give our body greatly affects our motivation, energy and happiness: Our life force, our mana, our drive to be better and best. I was missing this in my late 20's. I was eating for failure, not for success. I was feeding my body poisons, daily, like sugar and alcohol, thinking I was generally healthy with an occasional balanced "reward." In reality, I was actually, desperately seeking a happy mind and body. I was setting myself up for a cycle of frustration. But why? I was eating what I was told was healthy and balanced. I followed the food pyramid, and the advice of the " health experts," eating things with whole grains like bread, oatmeal, and lots of healthy fruit, attempting to achieve balance. Why wasn't it working? Why did I feel anything but balanced?

Rise and Shine

Eating foods, first thing in the morning, to spark our neurotransmitters like dopamine and acetylcholine will set you up for building your ultimate superhero self. Could it be this simple? It is. My mentor, Charles who coached hundreds of Olympians, developed the "meat and nuts breakfast" just for this purpose.

Dopamine

Breakfast and dopamine: By eating meats high in protein and essential amino acids, like red meat or even chicken or turkey, we spark healthy balances of dopamine. Dopamine is responsible for motivation and drive. If one skips breakfast, like Kendall did, and opts for a solo cup of coffee until noon, they risk setting their body chemistry up for failure. Worse, if they consume a high simple carbohydrate breakfast, they create an imbalance. They have a dopamine and serotonin spike then crash and are left craving these same foods a couple of hours later. I tell my new clients all of the time, that it is not their fault they are craving donuts at 10 am! They have chemically set themselves up for this by making the choice of a high carbohydrate breakfast. Much like a drug, they are left craving more and more, eventually becoming unable to be satisfied. This is the same thing that happens when drug addicts become saturated with dopamine and need more and more to achieve the same high. The hazardous result,

Morning run, 2019. Photo: Dave Albo

however, is that the more and more simple carbohydrates they eat, the more adipose and visceral fat tissue they end up with. This is a vicious cycle that can be halted with a better choice for the first meal of the day.[4] Dopamine, which comes from the anticipation of feeling good or reward, can be controlled by managing potential overstimulation of dopamine. By eating junk food all of the time, spiking the reward reaction, we create a tolerance to dopamine. That means we are then unable to have enough stores to access when we really need it: during exercise/performance. You know that feeling at the end of a race when you see the finish line and get a burst of energy? Scientists believe that is a neurotransmitter response—dopamine—not a physiological response![5]

According to studies, the best athletes have the highest dopamine levels.[6] You are an athlete. You are on your way to being a superhuman by optimizing your life.

Dopamine is also associated with risk. Risk can be a positive thing if it means you are willing to put yourself out there to achieve your greatest self. When was the last time you created an idea and followed through with it? It takes a certain amount of "risk" to be successful. It wasn't until I learned to eat for success that I had the motivation to compete. Dopamine is responsible for getting you out there on the track, or the court, or the field.

Dopamine is what allows you to have the confidence to believe you can do it and you can win! You may be just interested in beginning to exercise, or you may be a seasoned competitor. Either way you need motivation to start. And my advice: start where you are. Start now. Set yourself up for success by eating to spark your neurotransmitters in the morning. Eat for success and motivation.

Acetylcholine

The other neurotransmitter that is important to ignite is acetylcholine. Acetylcholine is derived from choline, which is found in nuts. It is also found in eggs, fish, red meat, and poultry. In general, to my clients, I do not recommend eggs every day for breakfast because the protein content is not high enough to achieve the nutrition goal I'm after for my clients' first meal. You see, the protein content of your first meal, and the first bites of your food in the morning should be high enough to stimulate your stomach acid. Your HCL, or stomach acid, is improved by a high protein diet.[7, 8] It is diminished by too many simple carbohydrates like breads and pastries. Many clients with acid reflux, irritable bowel and other gastrointestinal inflammations actually have too little stomach acid available to digest their food properly. The food sits undigested, causing the acid to flare back upwards. They are then, in turn put on antacids, which worsens the problem, since the original problem is not having enough acid! I have found a complete turn for the best when these clients start eating high quality animal protein, not plant-based protein,[9] as the first few bites of their meal and cutting grains, sugars, and legumes.

The latter, grains, sugar, and legumes, also have been shown to feed pathogenic gut bacteria, which can create gastrointestinal issues. Quality animal protein sources contain high amounts of glutamine and glycine which serve multiple functions, including healing the gut mucosal lining. The best amino acids for gut healing are all found in high quantities in animal protein.

In a comprehensive review of athletes and their gut bacteria, researchers discovered that those that ate high amounts of carbohydrates, low fat or high fiber and low fat (especially vegetarians and vegans), had an overabundance of the bacteria called *Prevotella*. As well, endurance trained athletes (marathon and ultra-distance running) had more *Prevotella* than short high intensity type athletes. Overexpression and overabundance of *Prevotella* is associated with almost every major disease including depression and several autoimmune diseases.[10] In other studies, high instances of *Prevotella* showed a direct correlation with lack of dopamine.[11] In contrast, those athletes that ate a diet high in animal protein had the prevalence of the bacteria type called Bacteroides. This type of bacteria is associated with more lean muscle mass and thwarting of pathogenic invaders (viruses etc.)[12]

Thus, by eating a few bites of say, grass fed beef, as your first meal of the day you are lighting the fire of the necessary chemical processes to absorb all of the essential nutrients you need like: zinc, magnesium, iron, etc. On the other hand, by starting with grains like a bagel, oatmeal, or even just coffee, you block absorption of these nutrients and decrease your neurotransmitters for motivation. I am not opposed to coffee, but in my preference for my clients, it should be kept to 1-2 cups, organic, percolated and come after you feed your body the correct fuel it needs to set up a successful day. Organic is preferred due to the high rates of pesticide use on coffee crops. Percolated, because it preserves the health benefits of terpene oils. After you eat so that the phytochemicals in it do not block the absorption of your nutrients and also so that it does not squash your appetite. You will feel better fueled throughout your day if you eat.

Acetylcholine carries brain signals among cells and activates the neurons in muscles. It plays a significant role in most major bodily systems, including cardiovascular, gastrointestinal/digestive contractions, bladder, respiratory

system, and parasympathetic nervous system. Acetylcholine is responsible, particularly, for learning and memory. In Alzheimer's disease, patients possess an abnormally low level of acetylcholine. The highest and most bioavailable (easily absorbed by the body) foods with choline, the precursor to making acetylcholine are: beef, chicken, fish, and eggs, followed by various seeds and nuts.

Protein

Although everyone's metabolic needs are different, I have found that generally, my clients thrive on a high protein, high "healthy fat" diet. Healthy fats can include a variety of foods including pasture-raised butter, grass-fed beef, most nuts, and coconut. Unhealthy fats include processed vegetable and seed oils, trans-fats and low quality greasy processed food. There are myths about high protein diets that are just that: fairytales by misaligned sources with an agenda. When I see hundreds of humans go from pale gray to sparkling superheroes, I know introducing more high-quality, animal protein is working!

Proteins are building blocks for our bodies. It is particularly important for those over 40 to increase their protein intake. Why? For one thing, we absorb less protein as we age. Instead of increasing protein, I see many people decreasing their protein as they age. Or, they replace it with less nutrient dense food. My mother is 80 years old. I introduced more meat and a high-quality protein shake a day to her. She lost 10 pounds in the first week of making this change because she was no longer hungry for sugar and junk food. She was satisfied with her food intake and her body started burning fat. She had more energy and her cognition was sharper. I love seeing my family and my clients thrive!

It is no coincidence that the Ancient Hawaiian kukini were said to eat mostly protein like rare-cooked chicken. They also ate fish and were not permitted to eat the dense carbohydrate rich local paste called poi. They avoided all "soggy foods."[13] I find it very interesting that the Hawaiian elite of the pre-missionary period focused on protein rich foods and avoided high carbohydrate/high fiber starches when training to become tall, muscular superhumans.[14]

Red Meat

One food that has gotten a bad rap over the years is red meat. I realize this section may be a dichotomy of 1. common sense for some: "Of course we should eat read meat" and 2. controversial for others, "What? I thought red meat was bad for you." I am sharing a special section on this fuel because it has single-handedly impacted the health of myself and my clients in a very positive way. Not everyone will have the same metabolic pathways, but I can say with confidence that by including high-quality red meat into the nutrition programs as a main component, my athlete clients and auto-immune clients have thrived.

Despite past and present attempts to vilify red meat, the most recent studies show that there is no evidence that red meat causes cancer or any other illness.[15] Our consumption of beef has declined since 1950 while the world's incidence of diabetes and obesity has steadily increased. Some are concerned about the environment. Ruminant animals, such as grazing cattle, can actually help rebuild the soil and take carbon out of our atmosphere.[16] In addition, by rebuilding the soil, grazing cattle offer a solution to the problem of soil exhaustion (crops strip the soil). It takes a much higher quantity of grains and more environmentally harmful transportation to ship these grains to create the same nutrient density that exists in red meat. You can see it and feel it yourself when a much smaller portion of steak is much more satiating than a bowl of cereal.

The idea of meat rotting in your stomach is also false. One doctor discovered that with normal stomach acid, patients with removed colons had no meat remnants in their colostomy bags. It had all been digested and absorbed prior to getting to the colon.[17] Not only that but animal protein is especially better digested than plant-based proteins like soy and pea protein. Those plant proteins were shown to produce fermented unpleasant byproducts, like ammonia, in the colon whereas animal protein was easier to digest and did not even make it as far as the colon.[18]

In my experience I have found red meat to be healing and beneficial to my clients. For me, personally, it has become my preferred fuel for sprinting. You read that correctly! I prefer to eat red meat almost daily and absolutely pre-competition. In fact, before all of my championship races, I eat grass fed steak. I pre-cook a high carnosine cut, like a loin cut, pack it in a container or baggie in a cooler bag and bring with me onto the field or warm up area. I chew the steak well, eating it about 1-1.5 hours prior to my race. Carnitine is important for transporting

fats to use as fuel. Using fats as fuel, instead of carbohydrates gives you a greater amount of energy. Plus, burning carbohydrates leads to the production of lactate in the muscles. By creating fat adaptation in the body, and feeding it carnitine prior to racing, you give it a second pathway for fuel. This does not happen in carbohydrate adapted bodies, or people who eat mostly carbohydrates for fuel. In fact, one study points out that eating carbohydrates prior to intense exercise inhibits using fat as fuel. Eating a high carbohydrate diet also increased the amount of blood lactate at the point of fatigue (you know, aka booty lock!)[19] Contrary to some thought, a high protein, high fat low carbohydrate diet does not negatively affect strength. Instead, a study of gymnasts pointed out that not only did they keep their strength but it was optimal for maintaining optimal weight and bodyfat.[20]

Carnosine also buffers lactic acid. Many people take the precursor to carnosine, called beta-alanine as a supplement before racing, however, the carnosine bioavailability in meat is much higher than in supplement form: 86% compared to 5-15% in supplements. Carnosine from beef becomes available in the bloodstream within15 minutes of consumption and is out of the bloodstream a few hours later, which is why I make sure to bring my grass-fed beef with me on the field or during warm-up.

The benefits of carnitine, carnosine, taurine, iron, zinc, B12 and folate (to name a few) create an optimal fuel for lean muscle mass, healthy hearts and holding on to muscle as we age. Recent studies show that even during the fastest part of the sprint, the first 10 seconds, the body can use the combination of carnitine and fat from red meat as fuel. Previously it was thought that only carbohydrates could fuel this part of a race. By eating a high-protein, high-fat meal before sprinting, you set your body up for ultimate success. The kukini certainly knew this, as rare chicken was also filled with carnitine, carnosine, taurine, and more!

We have a long history of finding out what works for athletes and what doesn't in scientific studies. Rarely, however, in this course of history have carnivore type athletes been studied. Dr. Shawn Baker, author of The Carnivore Diet is a great example of a warrior living and thriving on animal products alone. I can tell you, from my experience, firsthand, that my clients are excelling from consuming more high-quality, red meat. One diet does not fit all, but there are certain chemical reactions that can foster a more optimal human. Especially as we age, hacking into this biochemistry is extremely important. Someone once said, 'How can you eat a steak before a 400m? Why don't you carbohydrate load like everyone else?"

I replied, "How can you NOT eat a steak before a 400? It has all of the things I need to fuel me and buffer lactic acid. My body responds extremely well to running on red meat. Why would I eat grain and sugar filled carbohydrates when they make me tired, moody and nervous? Fructose is the culprit in everything from heart disease to obesity. And why, oh why, would I want to be like everyone else? I want to be better than everyone else!"

Telomeres

Another reason to increase protein as we age, is because as we get older we are subject to sarcopenia. Sarcopenia is the loss of muscle mass. If you are an athlete at any age, but especially over the age of 40, you need the building blocks to maintain muscle mass. Studies have shown, by having an adequate amount of lean muscle mass as you age, you counteract many of the biological aging processes. You can lengthen your telomeres, which are the caps on the ends of your DNA chromosomes, with proper nutrition and exercise. Simple sugary carbohydrates shorten these caps, which are like caps on the ends of your shoelaces, keeping your DNA from fraying and thus your cells from dying.[21] Protein and other nutrients can keep those telomeres intact. Not only that but protein, especially red meat, can actually lengthen them, giving a better quality of longevity.[22] We are living to be older and older on average, but the quality of this long life is dwindling with the increase of diseases like heart disease, cancer and Alzheimer's disease. The first step in creating your superhuman self, is to set yourself up, starting with the very first meal of your day, to grow into your superhuman self.

Just to think we regenerate EVERY cell in our body every ten years. A whole new set of bones in ten years? Wow! Some parts of our body are regenerated daily. Who do you want to regenerate into? I know I want to be the best, most optimal version of myself. I want to be the "Sister of Makoa!" Superhero mentality starts with igniting your day every day.

Let the Sun Shine!

Dopamine levels have been shown to be associated with Vitamin D levels. Vitamin D is important for nearly every bodily process and dictates how well we can handle stressors on our body. Vitamin D is depleted in people who live in areas with less sun, or longer winters. African Americans need more sun exposure to synthesize vitamin D and while 40 percent of the General population has been tagged as deficient, 76 percent of African Americans have found to be deficient. Of course, I have empowered myself and chosen to live in a place of paradise with sun year round. I am extremely grateful for this.

In Hawaiian mythology, it is the deity Kane that gives life force in the way of the dawn, or the sun. I echo the lessons of the ancients that came before me by suggesting that we wake and place ourselves in the energy of the sun, so that we may go forward in our day with life force.

Even in places of sunshine year round, people are covering up to avoid the scare of skin cancer. In my experience, small bouts of sunshine, especially in the early morning hours and 15-30 minutes during the middle of the day, without sunscreen are extremely beneficial to establishing strong circadian rhythms and getting a dose of vitamin D.

There are several things that block the absorption of vitamin D. These include: high fiber diets, plant-based proteins, pollution from cities, acid blocking drugs, gastric by-pass surgery, corticosteroid drugs like prednisone, and lack of enough stomach acid. Researchers discovered that animal protein sources and saturated fats were the best facilitators of increasing vitamin D stores.[23]

Our internal clocks, or circadian rhythms do more than govern our sleep/wake cycles. They are tied to almost all aspects of our gene expression, including hormone balance and energy. If you are feeling out of whack, your internal clock may be compromised.

Getting that dose of uninhibited Vitamin D every morning is crucial to promoting your superhuman self. Low Vitamin D has been tied to nearly every disease and illness out there and is essential for maintaining strong bone tissue. Whether it be cancer or the latest pandemic virus, high vitamin D levels are correlated with better health. Vitamin D deficiency can cause fatigue, muscle weakness, pain, depression, and weak bones. Those with darker skin especially need to make sure they get adequate Vitamin D because melanin does not absorb UV well. Consider getting your physician to check your Vitamin D level. If it is low, consider increasing animal protein foods and supplementation.

Even the early Polynesians recognized this. They used to say that those among them with darker skin from the sun had stronger bones. They felt pity for the fair-skinned Europeans when the explorers first sailed into Polynesian harbors on their ships. They thought the sailors were white with illness! Those that were darker were healthier with stronger bones. Why did they know this? The warring tribes would pick through the dead bodies on the war field, sifting through the corpses to make tools from the bones. The darker the skin, the stronger the bones and the stronger the tools.[24] Of course they were correct. Still to this day it is proven that those that have gotten the most sun, and have produced melanin in response as a natural sunblock, have stronger bone mineral density than their Caucasian counterparts.

Technology/Electronics

Less and less children are getting their adequate showering of sunshine due to excessive use of electronics. Lower dopamine has been associated with overuse of smartphones and other electronic devices. A few years ago, I sat on an airplane next to a high school principal. He was returning from a convention on dopamine depletion among high school students. The increased use of smartphones was contributing to a decrease in cognition, motivation and attentiveness among high school students.

The brain is most open to neuroplasticity, or learning new things in the first 25 years of life. This includes motor skills. However, neuroscientists have recently discovered that as we age, we can still keep our neuroplasticity going with a combination of: acetylcholine, dopamine, and long restful sleep (more on that later!) How could I run a faster 400m at age 43 than age 22? I check off all of these boxes.

As an athlete I make sure not to pick up my phone too much during the two weeks prior to a major competition. The checking of electronics, especially social media, gives a temporary hit of dopamine, in anticipation of the reward of attention. This might feel satiating at the time, but like a hit of sugar, continuously, it has long term effects on motivation and happiness. Dopamine depletion due to electronics has also been associated with teens and their sleep. Teens who stay up late on their phone are found to sleep worse and have more hormone imbalances.[25] The best idea is to avoid these small blasts of excitement/reaction (dopamine hits) in favor of real-life interactions with real-life people. You could even do a detox day or week when you don't pick up electronics at all. You will be surprised with how fast you feel better and less anxious. Meeting up with these real-life people, preferably outdoors in nature, will provide the type of balance and motivation you are perhaps lacking in your quest to become a superhero.

Kendall returned to me a month later, after changing her routine. Instead of a pale, sad face staring at me, I sat looking at sparkling eyes, (did you know that the neural components of our eyes are the only part of our actual brain that resides outside of our skull? Fascinating!) Vibrant, full of life, she was a shining person who had recently returned to exercise. She started rowing with a local canoe club. She felt refreshed and motivated to get up every morning to train on the beautiful ocean, sun shining. She found fellowship in the company of her team. She was thriving. Her happiness became my happiness as well.

Summary: 5 Ways To Ignite Your Day

1. Spark your neurotransmitters.

2. Protein… eat protein as your first bite of food and throughout the day to stimulate gastrin and HCL which promotes happiness by way of digesting food properly and balancing the body.

3. Telomeres: Eat to lengthen your telomeres. Avoid simple sugary carbohydrates and junk food.

4. Rise and Shine: Start your day with 10-30 min of sunshine without sunblock or covering.

5. Electronics/Technology: Avoid excessive use of electronics like phone, social media, emails, TV or internet news, etc.

Malaga, 2018. Photo: Dave Albo

Section II. Physical Peak (Body)

"E 'ai pono a e ho'oikaka kinono ke olakino maika'i."

Eat healthy and exercise for a healthy body.
(Olakino is the greatest wealth one can attain.)[26]

The Tale of Elei'o

Elei'o was a kukini runner for the king (ali'i) of Maui, Kakaalaneo. Kakaalaneo regularly sent Elei'o, his best and fastest runner to the other side of the island to get 'awa, or kava root. Elei'o was already legendary throughout the islands for his sprinting and distance running feats. Taking pride in the celebrity of his name, he began his journey with great swiftness.

Upon the way, he saw a beautiful woman up ahead. With all of his might, he sprinted toward her. But, alas, she was faster! She remained just further ahead of him, so that no matter how fast he sprinted, he could not "overtake" her. Intrigued and with perhaps a bit of hurt pride, he kept chasing her all the way to a village just past Kaupo, clear on the other side of the island.

Upon finally catching her, she said, "I am not mortal, but I am a spirit!" You see, Elei'o was not just a kukini, but also a kahuna, trained and gifted in the arts of medicine, ceremonies, and incantations. The spirit had attached to him to ask him to make her mortal again.

He obliged and after following her instructions to meet her family, who was housing her body, he renewed her spirit back into her body. She had also instructed him to have her family finish a fine feather cloak. The family, in such gratitude, finished the cloak and asked Elei'o to take their daughter, whose name was Kanikanilua (Kah-nee-kah-nee-lew-a) as his wife. Elei'o, being a humble warrior, said that her beauty was so great, she deserved to be queen. They began their journey back to Lahaina to present her to his ali'i.

After a slower journey to Lahaina, because she was no longer a fast spirit, they arrived and Elei'o hid Kanikanilua in the bushes. As he approached, the king's men seized him and ordered that he be burned in the imu fire for disappearing and not returning fast enough according to the King's bidding.

Elei'o walked through the fire unharmed. The king confronted him and asked how it was that he escaped unharmed, at which point Elei'o presented the feather cloak, said to be the first of the Hawaiian feather cloaks of the kings, and told the king what had happened. He called for Kanikanilua and when the king saw her, he was so taken with her beauty, he indeed made her his queen.

Illustration by CM Monteleone

The tale of Elei'o, passed down through generations, was written down in the late 1800's. Over time, the feather cloak has become a symbol of royalty in Hawaiian culture. I find it suiting that the first of these cloaks was laid not upon a king, but a runner. Kai Markel, compliance manager for the Office of Hawaiian Affairs, described the cloaks as "an ahu (altar) on the shoulders of the sacred ali`i" (chiefs). The deity status of the capes speaks to this tale of Elei'o who can race a spirit and perform the magic of reinvigorating a dead body into a beautiful woman. I take inspiration from Elei'o as he was a superhero—he even had a cape—and he was a runner, but even more so I take inspiration from the idea that he gave life back to a body. Bring new energy and strength to the body and joining it with the spirit is what I look to do with my clients.

Time and again I witness the demise of the best laid plans for exercise. Back in present day Lahaina, I met with Leilani, a spritely, wavy-haired firecracker, who reached out to me, frustrated because she was eating and exercising according to what she thought would help her lose weight. She was not losing weight, however, despite drinking "healthy" fruit smoothies daily before or after her long cardio sessions. She ran on the treadmill or biked for one hour 5 days a week and was not losing weight. How could this be? The only thing Leilani seemed to be losing was precious time. Over an hour of her day wasted with no results.

Often, people are told to incorporate massive amounts of long slow "cardio" into their daily routine for cardiovascular health. Not only does this turn out to be boring, but is usually detrimental to overall health instead of positive for their biomarkers. Why? Well, frequently, the process of starting is hard. Diving into running long distance, for instance, often leads to overuse injury and sometimes sheer boredom. Second, it is hard for busy folks to fit in long periods of cardio into their day. Not everyone has time to dedicate long sessions on a road, bike, or treadmill. Third, long bouts of cardio do not lead to healthy biomarkers, thwarting disease. Sometimes, they even lead to holding more body fat than cutting body fat.[27]

Optimal body fat percentage, especially elimination of visceral fat, is important to encouraging quality of longevity in life. It has been my experience that this is best and most efficiently achieved through high-intensity exercise in intervals. My favorite form, as you might imagine, is sprinting. Dr. Sean O'Mara is a specialist in "Human Optimization." He has received a grant to measure visceral fat around our organs via a special scan. He is a huge advocate for sprinting, especially as we age. His results speak volumes. Compared with plant based, long distance runners, meat-eating sprinters have less visceral fat in his detailed MRI scans.

Sprinting in short intervals for at least 20 minutes has also been shown, in comparison with distance running, to increase BDNF more. BDNF is Brain-Derived-Neurotrophic-Factor. This means, subjects had a greater capacity to learn information. When tested, they were 20 percent better at answering questions. Their cognition was sharper. This a major breakthrough in combating Alzheimer's as we age. It appears high intensity sprints could make us smarter and keep our minds firing brightly. Why?[28]

It is speculated that a group of neurotransmitters called catecholamines are responsible for the great fat burning results of high intensity sprinting. These neurotransmitters include: epinephrine, (adrenaline), norepinephrine, and dopamine! If you are sensing a pattern here, you are on the correct path. Studies have shown that these are more active post sprinting, than post distance running. As a result, scientists discovered that sprinting, as opposed to distance running can make you not only smarter, but happier by curbing anxiety.[29] Because they are more active post sprinting, your body keeps burning fat as fuel long after your workout is finished as it is still reaching to replace the oxygen debt which occurred while sprinting.[30] So you burn more fat longer after the shorter sprint workout. Not only that, but the neurotransmitters are the same ones that are associated with neuroplasticity (cognition, learning, and motor skills) as we age.

So instead of training for a marathon, a more efficient way to burn both subcutaneous (outside) belly fat AND visceral (inside surrounding the organs) belly fat, is to start sprinting.

1. SPRINTING/DYNAMIC EXERCISE

Sprinting seems daunting to most. And, well, it should be in a way. I never encourage just strapping on some spikes and going all out on a track. The best way to be FAST OVER 40, or at any age, is to take it slow! Take it slow starting. Take it slow strength training. Take it slow recovering. Take it slow eating. Did you think that would be the advice for being fast? To be slow?

Be dynamic! Start your sprint training with a dynamic warm up which is the opposite of static stretching. I include my favorite dynamic warm up in the appendix of this book. Static stretching, or holding your stretch for a long period of time, has, in my experience been the opposite of beneficial. I had an amazing speed development coach, named Dale Upton, help me to develop a great dynamic warm up. Dynamic means that you do not hold your stretches, but instead, you move continuously into your stretches. Your muscles are elastic. If you keep stretching them further and further like a rubber band, you encourage that rubber band to become thin and worn. This leads to increase in muscle tears and other soft tissue injuries. It is especially important for sprinting that you keep the elasticity in your muscle by warming up with movement. By executing a dynamic warm up, you avoid stretching the muscles too much too thin and you also encourage the maintenance and development of fast twitch fibers in your muscles. Both of those are necessary for your superhuman sprint!

Although we are each born with genetic predispositions to move with fast (Type 2) or slow (Type 1) twitch fibers, we can change this through training just as the kukini did. In general, due to hormones, males possess more fast twitch fibers than females, making them naturally faster. Fast twitch fibers are encouraged during a warm up that remains dynamic and does not include jogging. One of the effective ways to get slower at any fast twitch sport is to run slow, long distances. If you want to run fast, keep your training fast. If you are a serious athlete in sprinting or other fast twitch activities, I also highly recommend training at sea level. Training at altitude, after only a short time (within two weeks) promotes the transition of fast twitch fibers to slow.[31] If you are starting your journey into sprinting, start for one month with just the warm up before continuing to the next step.

Step two in beginning sprinting, especially over age 40, is to find a hill. Hill walking and running will force you into proper sprinting form, even if you have no clue of how to do sprinting drills. Your foot will be, what we call, dorsi-flexed (toe up). Your calves and quadriceps will be activated and your power will be developed. Remember to take it slow and not to rush it so as

Feeling like a warrior, 2019
Photo: J. Anthony Martinez

to prevent injury! I often have clients that just walk the hill for a month before jogging.

If you have something to measure, measure out 200 meters or 656.17 feet. If you do not have anything to measure with, not to worry! Time yourself walking up the hill at a moderate pace for 2:45-3 minutes. Begin this phase by walking the hill as many times as you can up to 10 times. If you are already a runner, you may slowly jog up the hill working up to 10 times, walking back down for your rest period. Perform this workout once per week, timing yourself as you go up the hill. If you are new to running, only walk up it for the first month. Then, progress to jogging.

As the months go by, you should notice that you are getting faster running up the hill. I suggest leaving the smart phone at home and buying a regular old timing watch. Electromagnetic frequency while exercising is not great for the muscle tissue. Music, while ok to listen to beforehand to increase dopamine, can be distracting during the focus part of a workout. As my mentor used to say, "They don't play your favorite song during your race, do they?" It is better to focus on the task at hand and allow your senses to feel what is going on. The sights and sounds of the world are important to our balance. I am also not a fan of microwaving your brain with Bluetooth, so leave the phone at home and the airpods buried forever.[32] In fact, I ask my athletes to avoid wireless as much as possible and to never touch their phones to their heads or their bodies to avoid disruption of tissue and hormones.[33]

After you have sufficiently mastered hills and you are strong enough to run fast on a flat surface, you can find a field and measure out 30 meters, 50 meters and 100 meters. A regular hardware store should have a measuring wheel. Running on a soft surface, like a field, is kind to your shins, although they should be already getting sufficiently conditioned from your gradual hills. Try to find a field with smooth grass so you are not likely to twist an ankle in a hole.

If you do not have access to a measuring tape or wheel, try running for 8-10 seconds and walking back for a total of 20-minute exercise time.

Next, progress from field running to track running after one month. You can start in a standing position or, as you get faster, in a 3-point start. (See 3-point start in the appendix.) You want to concentrate on driving off of the balls of your feet, feeling the power of each stride increasing until you reach your maximum velocity. I encourage you to stay in well supported, flat running shoes for at least a month or two before attempting sprint spikes. Sprint spikes are amazing for really encouraging grabbing the track with the balls of your feet in the drive phase, but they don't possess much support for your feet. It is better to slowly condition your body to be balanced, strong and stable before introducing spikes. When you are ready for spikes, you will find many different brands with different fits. It takes time and experience to find which spikes fit your foot type best. For beginners, I usually recommend one with extra support like Saucony.

Once on the track, there are various sprint workouts you can do from here, which I will also include in the appendix. I am biased toward the 400m sprint training because it encompasses all 3 energy systems and lactic training is the best way to lose bodyfat. Those energy systems are: 1. ATP/Creatine Phosphate 2. Lactate: the second phase when oxygen runs out and blood lactate is produced 3. Endurance: the final is a touch of the sprint endurance phase. It is my belief that sprint training that incorporates all 3 energy systems, like 400m training, leads to the fastest way to optimal biomarkers of health and happiness. By starting slow and increasing as you develop your strength and speed you will find a new level of human optimization/superhero mentality.

2. STRENGTH TRAINING

Tempo
Strength training, or lifting weights is extremely important for any age. I am lucky to have some really awesome mentors in the strength coaching world. Strength training will help you develop lean muscle mass in order to be functionally strong in life (i.e. lift a bag of heavy groceries), prevent injury when exercising/sprinting, and thwart sarcopenia, a natural decrease in muscle mass as we age. Dr. Gabrielle Lyon has done some amazing work in "muscle-centric medicine" and she points out that our muscle tissue is

our organ of longevity. It impacts our hormones, our metabolic processes and more.[34]

Proper strength training techniques to encourage muscle mass for fast twitch fibers, injury prevention and health are not as hard as you might think. In this area, I am also a big fan of moving slow. Being a student of Charles Poliquin, I am an advocate of incorporating tempo training. Tempo training means you do not have to move massive amounts of weight at a fast velocity down and up. Rather, you can concentrate on proper form during your lift while moving the weight slowly in the eccentric position to recruit more muscle fibers and develop strength with lower amounts of weight to start.

If you are a beginner to lifting weights, I strongly recommend hiring a strength coach that is familiar with Poliquin's work. Strength programs should be tailored to each individual and should correct individual prior injuries/imbalances for optimal strengthening of weaknesses. That being said, I will include a couple of beginning strength programs to get started on building muscles to support sprinting. Always check with your physician before trying new exercise programs.

Plyometrics

A component of strength training that should be included after stabilizing muscles are strengthened through lifting weights is plyometrics. Just like the other parts of becoming FAST OVER 40, take plyometrics slow. Start with just a few exercises and build every week. I remember when I first started doing plyometrics, I could barely jump at all. I was certainly not as strong as our hero, Elei'o. I was holding baby weight in my midsection and thighs and I felt like a monk seal trying to jump over a fence. After time and dedication, however, I was able to get better and better as I became stronger and stronger. The key is to be consistent. Show up and work on it a little at a time. Included in the appendix is a suggested plyometric/core workout that can be done at home or at the track once a week. It is simple. If you feel you cannot complete it all the first time, no worries! Just start and complete as much as you can.

3. SLEEP

Can you believe scientists still do not know why we sleep? Of course, there are speculations and guesses but the act of putting ourselves in such a vulnerable state to the rest of the world, for so many hours (particularly in ancient times with predators roaming about) seems counter to survival. Yet, we know that we cannot survive without sleep.

We know more and more that we cannot thrive without sleep either! To be a superhero, to be a superhuman, to optimize our human self, we need proper sleep.

Be very wary of those that brag about how little sleep they get. This has been proven to be something that has detrimental effects on our health. For instance, Alzheimer's disease, which is marked by an increase in amyloid beta plaque in our brains, is associated with bad sleep. Even after one night of bad sleep, more of this plaque builds. In the last 10 years, it has been discovered that we have a system in our brain called the glymphatic system. The glymphatic system, much like the lymphatic system removes waste, but while the lymphatic system removes metabolic wastes from our system, the glymphatic system removes it from our brain. It appears to be most active in the later hours (post 6 hours) of sleep, and is crucial to removing the amyloid beta plaque buildup, and creating neuroplasticity in our brains. Neuroplasticity is responsible for learning new things, being creative, and learning new motor skills (like sprinting). All of the hard work done in the day is remembered and stored during long, restful sleep. I cannot stress enough the importance of this to the equation. Getting long restful sleep allows our body to complete necessary repair procedures for our minds and muscles.[35]

For athletes (remember, you are an athlete now!), sleep is crucial for boosting testosterone, which enhances athletic performance, even in women. It has also been demonstrated that a minimum of 8 hours of sleep is necessary for injury prevention in athletes. In a study, 6 hours of sleep was associated with a 70 percent higher risk of injury. The risk dropped with each hour of sleep with 9 hours being barely there.[36]

Photo: J. Anthony Martinez

Not only that, data shows, athletes indicated a decrease in vertical jump ability after disrupted/poor sleep. Vertical jump ability and sprinting are directly correlated. In order to be your most powerful superhuman self, you must get adequate sleep!

Suggestions For Better Sleep:

1. Avoid junk food (processed food with artificial ingredients).

2. Eat a diet high in bioavailable zinc like oysters, and red meat, as zinc deficiency is associated with poor sleep. FYI zinc deficiency is also correlated with Alzheimers. Coincidence? I think not! [37] [38]

3. Sleep in a temperature of about 68 degrees.

4. Sleep with your room dark like a cave.

5. Avoid all electronics for a minimum one hour before bedtime. Read a book instead.

6. Turn off Wifi in the house. Electrical signals from Wifi have been shown to disrupt sleep. [39]

7. Sleep with phone on airplane mode and outside of the room or at least 10 feet away. You can have your alarm on without the signal or just get an old-fashioned alarm clock if you need it. Note: alarm clocks are not great for waking up as they cause body chemical distress! Try to wake up naturally on time daily. If you get adequate, restful, sleep you should be able to do this.

8. Avoid alcohol and marijuana before bed. Both are toxins that make it difficult for all of your bodily processes to recover. Contrary to belief, just because they are sedatives, they do not help you sleep better. Restlessness and poor sleep spike a few hours after falling asleep and people tend to become dependent on these crutches for falling asleep. [40]

9. Make sure you are not magnesium deficient and consider taking a supplement with Magnesium L-Threonate or Inositol. [41] This type of magnesium has been found to

elevate the amount of magnesium circulating in your brain resulting in less loss of dopamine neurons and better motor skills.[42] I generally do not encourage melatonin as a supplement to my clients, as melatonin tends to decrease your body's own ability to make melatonin which is important for keeping internal clocks, or circadian rhythms intact.

10. Eliminate all distractions to sleep. If your cat wakes you up every night, put the cat out. Your health and well-being are the most important priority in your life. To be superhuman you must control your environment to the best of your ability. I often encourage safe co-sleeping for the moms of newborns because this eliminates the distraction of waking up to walk to the baby crying. If the baby is there and ready to feed, they don't cry in distress and everyone gets better rest.

11. Eat a satisfying high protein, high healthy fat meal a couple of hours before bed. An addition of carbohydrates is also better in the evening than the morning as carbohydrates make you sleepy. It is important not to eat right before bed as the digestion process is best sitting or standing upright. Laying down after eating a big meal can cause gastrointestinal distress and promote bad sleep.

12. Do not exercise right before bed. Exercise causes a spike in cortisol, the stress hormone. It takes some time to bring this back down and you will not sleep well if you are trying to go to sleep with high cortisol. On the other hand, regular exercise, performed earlier in the day, is associated with better sleep cycles.[43]

13. Keep a Grateful Log. Keeping a grateful log helps you go to sleep with a positive mindset.

4. RECOVERY

One of the fastest ways to get off track from our goal of being a superhero is to save the world too many times. Even superheroes need a break. In order to repair your muscles and allow your body to repair itself, you cannot be ripping it apart over and over without a break. Think of the fibers in your muscles and how awesome it is that they tear apart when you run or strength train, only to be woven back together stronger! Such a miracle! Now think of those fibers being constantly ripped without enough time to repair and get stronger. Your body starts to recognize this as a stress. It produces more and more stress hormones, or cortisol, leading to adrenal fatigue. Soon, your energy and performances are hitting a plateau, then declining. Excessive long distance running as you age can also promote stress on your body through an increase in ROS (Reactive Oxygen Species) as well as poor gut lining health. This is another reason I am an advocate of sprinting or short durations of high intensity training as we age.[44] These ROS, while during exercise are necessary (read: don't take antioxidants while training!), are damaging to our cells afterward. Short duration athletes like sprinters, could supplement with antioxidants in non-training hours to mitigate ROS. However, endurance athletes did not show the same response.[45] I know plenty of people that love to run distance and compete in triathlons, however, according to the science, perhaps it is time for sprinting to be the new trend in healthy exercise.

To avoid overtraining, take rest days. Just how many rest days will be dictated by age and level of activity. Generally, my schedule looks something like this: MWF run in the morning around 8:30 am, then strength train around 5-6 pm. Off from all training on Tue, Thurs and Sunday. Upper body strength training on Sat. morning. This allows me to have time to rest my body and recover to come back strong for my workouts. Other professional athlete clients of mine train M, Tue, off Wed., Train Thurs, Fri. Off Sat./Sun. If you have a competition schedule, attempt to train similar to your schedule. For instance, if it looks like you will race on Saturdays, run your faster sprint workout on Saturdays.

When approaching major competitions, I back off of the strength training for a week or so. This means I decrease my workout, not my load and adjust my plan. Women are less likely to peak with 1-2 weeks of totally off strength training. Men are shown to peak with 1 week completely off.[46] In strength training you can also train in cycles. Some people vary their cycles bi-weekly and some train 3 weeks on and one week off. It is up to you and how you feel and what your goals are. The main thing is to make sure to get some recovery, sometime, somewhere. Signs of overtraining include excessive fatigue and declining performance.

One of the best ways to make sure your body recovers, is to feed it well. As an athlete (you are a superhero athlete now) you need proper nutrients to build a strong body. Again, I am an advocate of eating: high protein, high healthy fat, low carbohydrate, very low sugar, grain free, no artificial ingredients. I have seen this type of fueling take mediocre athletes and build them into machines of athletic destruction. They are absolutely shredding their old personal bests with new fervor, energy and exuberant strength. Why? Their nutrition is optimal for expression of genes to get them to the next level.

Post workout is the best time to consume protein because our cells are more open to absorbing it then. If you are tolerant to whey, I recommend a high-quality, grass-fed whey protein[47] with no artificial ingredients for post workout recovery. Whey protein has been shown to blunt cortisol (stress hormone), help repair muscle tissue and even helps replenish the glycogen stores in your muscle tissue. Intaking a lower carbohydrate level soy protein, on the other hand, did not blunt cortisol as effectively, and additionally lowered testosterone. Considering testosterone is an important muscle and speed-producing hormone for both men and women, I do not recommend plant-based proteins which are devoid of the essential amino acid called leucine.[48]

You might think that winning a gold medal at a World Championship would be the highlight of my athletic career. Number one in the world! Wow! Yet, even better than when I won the gold medal at age 43, was running a faster time than I did 22 years earlier in college. What was the difference? I had an outstanding coach then and one now. The training was great then and great now. The difference was the nutrition. By knowing what to eat to spark neurotransmitters, sleep well, recover, build strength and encourage speed, I was able to change my genetic expression to become an even stronger, faster human than my peak age of my early 20's. I barely paid any attention to my nutrition in my college days. I look back now and see the mistakes I made. Now, more important than ever, I learn to eat according to what makes me strongest, fastest and with the best bloodwork my doctor has ever seen. My passion is to be my optimal self in order to thrive and take care of my family and clients. My passion is to have my clients thrive in health and happiness so that they too can take care of their loved ones. Even better than 10 gold medals or a lifetime personal best in running is when a client says to me that I changed their life through my encouragement in nutrition and exercise. That is the ultimate reward.

After meeting Leilani, who was stuck unable to lose weight, I changed her whole program. Since she had some fatty tissue on her liver, I took her off of excess fruit in her eating plan—meaning I had her ditch the daily smoothie. Fructose has long been associated with fatty liver. Fat tissue deposits on the liver, as a result of overconsumption of carbohydrates and alcohol, can contribute to numerous disease states and weight gain. In fact, we have known since Ancient Egypt that eating grains such as wheat and corn along with high fructose fruits have fattened the livers of mammals. This is where foie gras, or fattened goose liver delicacy was born! The Romans perfected it with addition of honey, wine and figs. While everyone is metabolically different, I have found that those clients holding body fat in certain areas thrive when they eliminate excessive high-fructose fruits.[37] I really enjoy individually assessing each client's personal metabolic needs and giving them a specific plan to meet their goals.

Leilani trashed her smoothies for steak and started to strength train and sprint. Her metabolism shifted to learn to oxidize fat for fuel. Her body fat began to melt off, her energy level increased and because sprinting didn't take up as much time as long steady cardio, she had more time to spend working on her passions. She now loves her body, feels happy and confident and has gotten rid of the fatty liver!

Make sure to get adequate animal-based protein and nutrient-dense foods to thrive as a superhero!

5. NATURE/BALANCE

An important component of recovery is getting into nature. In Hawaiian legends and culture, the harmony with life and nature is one. Just like the balance of everything down to microorganisms, we must adhere to honoring our environment by interacting with nature. On your recovery days or even on your exercise days, try to get into nature as much as you can. The energy gained when getting away from industrial society with all of its pollutants and technology is key to balance. Our bodies are electrical currents. The body's frequency changes with too many electrical elements surrounding us. Things like wi-fi, cell signals, air conditioning, television, etc. in excess disrupt our frequency. A secret to being superhuman is to increase your "negative ions" which are a good thing despite the word "negative." They are molecules found in abundance in places like mountain streams, waterfalls, oceans, and thunderstorms. Do you ever feel recharged after a thunderstorm? It could be the negative ions! I am a big believer in getting your bare feet on the ground and getting outdoors as much as possible.

The immense types of micro bacteria in our environment are also beneficial to us. Research has proven that children who grow up outdoors in rural environments have a greater diversity of bacteria and stronger immune systems.[38] Having a strong immune system at any age, during this time in our world of foreign toxins and viruses is extremely important.

I am fortunate to be able to live next to a mountain stream, only a mile or so from the ocean. Here on Maui we are very far removed, being part of an archipelago sitting by itself in the middle of the Pacific Ocean. Maui is a truly special place as one can feel the energy coming from this great source of natural balance. This could be why the visitors to Maui say they feel it is a "healing" place. I believe this to be true and its precious nature helps me heal and recover my body on my off days, helping me to balance and become my optimal self. Identify your closest source of nature and get into it.

Reducing Toxins from our environment can be hard, especially if you live in a city. Toxins are stored in our fat cells and can sometimes cause hormone imbalance by mimicking things like estrogens in our cells.[39] A quick way to reduce toxins would be to eliminate all fragrances from your world. Sharpen your super senses by getting rid of air fresheners, detergents with fragrance, chemical filled hair products and styling products. Choose paraben and sulfate free options, with no artificial fragrance. Essential oils, if used occasionally, are usually fine in products or for cleaning, etc.

I am known to replace my clients' lotion with organic coconut oil. I instruct them to apply it after they shower. Coconut oil is great for the skin and has antimicrobial and antibacterial properties. In Hawaii the coconut is the tree of life, the great provider, called the "kumu nui." A local coconut farmer, Kai, speaks of this "great source" in Polynesian culture as giving balance. He farms his coconuts to honor this balance by using agricultural methods that rely on microbacterial organisms to fertilize and act as pesticides instead of artificial ones. We discussed how we, as humans need this balance in our micro-organisms as well, to act against foreign invaders. By keeping a good microbiome inside and outside, we keep pathogens (bad bacteria, viruses, parasites, etc) at bay.

Even more recently, the local coral reef in some areas, had been overrun by invasive algae. Scientists gave the reef some probiotics to successfully restore health and balance. We can see this algae as a metaphor for the overgrowth of certain bacteria in our gut. We need the balance, just like the reef does.[40]

The island around me provides lessons in balance consistently. Coconut oil is a great way to protect your skin while being natural to the environment around you and in you. It is such great armor that even after swimming in the ocean, I see the water beading up on the outside of this awesome protective barrier. I highly recommend it, as our skin is an organ which soaks up what we put on it. I advise against feeding it toxins and rather feed it a food safe to eat and good for micro-balance.

Top 5 Practices for an Olakino Maika'i Healthy Body

1. Sprinting   2. Strength Training   3. Sleep
4. Recovery   5. Nature/Balance

Section III. Self/Soul

"Mahalo i ka mea i loa'a."

Be thankful for what you have.

Horse Racing

Illustration by CM Monteleone

One day a ship arrived at the Big island, and the white Europeans introduced what they believed was a great gift to the Hawaiian king—horses. What was the purpose of this large dog-looking creature, the Hawaiian's wondered. The white men explained it could run much faster and longer than any human, able to deliver information, letters, and goods at amazing speeds.

One proud kukini, who believed very powerfully in his training and in his name, challenged a race with these new horses. With full confidence in his own strength and name, he went to the line with the horse... and won!

The Hawaiians were less than impressed with these horses. They had all they needed in their kukini. When war would threaten them, the kukini would run to the villages warning them to prepare. Paul Revere may have ridden a horse, but the kukini just used their own two very fast feet.

The Race.

The best way to achieve superhuman, superhero status is to know that you are one. You are an athlete. You are a superhero, even if you may not feel like it just yet. Your self-image and your belief in self is an integral part of your health and happiness. Believe in yourself, your name and your power, and become a legend and a superhuman.

1. Self Image/Self Confidence

What is your self image? If you aren't sure, start writing down what you want to see yourself as. If you see yourself as weak, full of fear or panic and incapable, that is likely what you currently are or will become. I challenge you to change that image this instant. Give yourself the power to believe you can become the impossible. You can be a sprinter over the age of 40, or any age! You can be a World Champion. You can inspire others to be their best selves. This vine of positivity, health, and happiness can grow from me to you to many others through this book. Make it happen!

Do not become fearful that others will judge you as arrogant for your self image. This is a mistake many humans make. They are fearful of what others might think of them. Your opinion of yourself is way more important than anyone else's. They don't know you. YOU know you. A key component to champion mentality is to wash away mistakes of the past and treat them as lessons for the future.

Anthony, a strong professional athlete, top in the country in his sport, was having trouble making progress. A few things were going on in his life that were preventing him from getting adequate sleep. His stress measurements were so out of proportion, I knew something was going on personally with him. After he shared his story with me, I told him that he needed to let go of what should have been or what could have been. Let go of any past mistakes in his personal life or in his sport that he may have made. True champions see their mistakes as a part of the process to succeed, not a reason to keep failing. If you dwell on your mistakes, you are likely to keep making them. Instead, if you false-start, for example, think about why you did, make a plan for not doing it again in the future and then forgive yourself. FORGIVE YOURSELF. Too many people drown in a sticky pool of guilt and never

Feeling confident at the start of the 200m finals in Torun, Poland at the World Championships, 2019.

move forward. It matters not if others have forgiven you for your mistake. This is not their journey. This is your life adventure and in order to become a superhero, you must allow your star to shine. Be guarded against anyone who tries to steal that shine in any way.

Instead of listening to outside voices, own who you are (your superhero identity) and become that person. Sometimes we can relate to fictional superheroes in stories. I love promoting Wonder Woman Wednesday and wearing blue shorts with stars, a red sports bra and red compression socks. I find that by empowering myself to feel like a superhero, it in turn empowers others to have the confidence to do the same. By being confident in who you are and your superhuman, superhero self image, you are now giving power to others to do the same. It's like magic!

Tell yourself that you are the kind of person who …. Fill in the blank. Me? I'm the kind of person who honors my body and becomes strong and fast. I am the kind of person who is number one in the world. I am the kind of person who is gracious and giving to others, etc. Become the superhero. Anthony went on to accept any past mistakes that he actually did or that someone else thought he did and moved on. He shed others' opinions of him and channeled his own self image of being the best in his sport. By moving on and focusing on his goals of the future, instead of the past, he went on to become even stronger and win National and International competitions.

2. Love

You might be thinking…What's love got to do with it? What's love got to do with being FAST OVER 40? By finding balance in all areas of life, you will thrive in all areas. You must ask yourself if you are able to love other people. I found the greatest love of my life, here on Maui when I presented a self-image as instructed above and stated what I wanted in my relationships. I now have very loving relationships with not only my husband, but also my family, my friends, and my community. By encouraging love with a confident self, you replace fear with strength. You believe in the impossible and therefore are able to achieve your optimal superhero self with a foundational support from others whom you love and love you back. This support is very important to providing a solid structure on which to build your goals. By loving your fellow human being, you encourage that love to be returned and thus new doors to new levels will open for you to reach your best self.

3. Meditation/Prayer

There's no way you will reach your own human optimization without taking time to disconnect from the noise of society and listen to yourself. Whether it is through meditation or prayer, listen to yourself. Listen to your thoughts and needs. Remember your self-care will lead to the care of others. This is a foundational concept found in many ancient religions. Buddhist monks often call themselves "selfish Buddhists" because they know that by meditating and giving to others, they feel happier and better, thus it becomes self-care. Meditation also changes our neurotransmitters and brain waves. If you have never mediated before it is easy to start. Begin by sitting quietly by yourself, listening to your thoughts. If you find yourself saying, I don't have time to sit by myself for a few minutes, then you REALLY need meditation!

Try to change any negative thoughts to positive ones. Instead of "complaining" to yourself about something being broken, or complaining maybe you don't have something etc, change it to : I am thankful I have_____. I love_____. Eventually you can push thoughts out completely and repeat one word over and over for a few minutes to unwind from your own mind. If you find this difficult, no worries! Just concentrate on visualizing your best self. See yourself in the place you want to be.. See yourself in the clothes you love. Since you are an athlete now, see yourself executing your race or match to perfection, winning every time. Keep visualizing during your quiet time. If you are spiritual in organized religion, you can pray to your deity or God. Praying is a great way of thanking your God for what you have and pinpointing what you want. By asking for something in a prayer you can visualize your best most optimal self.

My family, Photo: J. Anthony Martinez

Example; "Dear God, please let me win my race; Dear God, please let me stay happy and healthy for my family." Always keep it positive and thankful.

Stress is a natural part of growth. In order to get better and be our best warrior version of ourselves we must not eliminate stress, but instead, strive to manage it. By meditation and shifting our frame of perception of the event that is causing stress, we can change "distress" into "eustress. Distress is damaging, whereas eustress is beneficial. Distress suppresses our immune system. Eustress supports it. Distress causes our blood vessels to constrict in anticipation of a physical attack. Eustress, when we perceive a positive outcome to the challenge ahead of us, can increase our cardio output. In college, prior to a race, I would get anxiety. Now that I eat a diet rich in B12 and folate, which protect my myelin (neural) sheaths, and I reframe my mind to think positive and believe in myself, I change distress to eustress. I use the excitement to my advantage!

4. Grateful Log

One of the best things I learned from my mentor was to keep a grateful log. I have all of my clients, especially my Olympians and professional athletes, do this. This is how the grateful log goes:

1. In the morning, in a notebook, write down what you are thankful for BEFORE it has happened to you. It can be big or small. Example: "I am thankful I had a peaceful, productive day." Or "I am thankful I broke the world record." Really get creative and make it anything you want. Anything is possible!

2. In the evening recite or write the following: (my family takes turns reciting at the dinner table)
    - Who did I help today? (If you didn't help anyone you have some inner work to do to become a superhero. Hello? Everyone knows superheroes help!)
    - Who helped me today? (If no one helped you, you are really a jerk and you definitely need to work on yourself to become a superhero!)
    - What did I learn today? This is extremely important because you should always be learning. In fact in order to become an optimal

My Superhero Family , 2019
Photo: J. Anthony Martinez

human in anything you do, you must keep up with learning about it. Instead of listening to the narrative of "what people say" or listening to crappy news channels, find out for yourself. Always ask questions from those who have excelled in the field you are interested in professionally or athletically. I am going to venture to say you have learned a thing or two from reading my experiences. Good job! Keep learning and keep asking questions.

- What am I grateful for? This one is pretty self-explanatory. Just remain grateful for what you have instead of being sad or complaining about what you don't have. If anything you have learned that you have the power to have anything you want if you put your superhero mind to it!

5. Give Back

The final element for developing your champion spirit and balancing to become Fast over 40 or a superhero in life, is giving back. It never fails that each time I give to someone, it comes back double. I give without expectation of return. I have given money, even when I have not had much money left. I give my time. I give my talent. There is one thing that you, personally, are already a superhuman at more than the average person next to you. What is it? I am blessed to be gifted at many things. One of them is art. Sometimes I volunteer to teach a painting class to kids, or paint a mural at a local school, no charge. I identify my talents, what I have to offer and I give it. I give to my community by doing community service in the way of landscaping (which is not a talent of mine, but is needed) and by coaching. If I need money, it never fails to donate. The universe seems to return the finances two-fold before I know it.

I encourage you to put the final touch on becoming a champion and becoming a superhero, by giving back whenever you can. This will help you establish and build that community foundation that will help you to be at your best, most optimal self in all aspects of health and happiness!

In Hawaii we are taught to constantly spread love and gratitude through the tradition of Aloha. We live on small islands and how we treat each other is important.

5 Things to Promote Spirit

1. Self Image/Self Confidence
2. Love
3. Meditation/Prayer
4. Grateful Log
5. Give Back

Conclusion

The last king of Hawaii, David Kalakaua had a kukini by the name of Antone Kaoo. He was nicknamed the "Great Old Horse of Wailua." The newspaper articles about him from around 1910, talk about his great sprinting skills. He also trained for fast running all the way up to the 15-mile run. Legends of Hawaiian culture like these, really inspired others to take up running and training.

It is my hope that by recounting the experiences of my journey, from going from an average mom of three kids who did not run for 20 years, to a Team USA World Champion and running faster than I did in college, will inspire you.

There are many ways to achieve health and happiness. The success of my own story and my clients' stories are like the stars in the sky. We are shining bright to light the way for you to do the same. Go shine bright my friends, to light the way for others!

Many Blessings to you on your journey! Aloha Nui Loa!

With my daughter, a great source of inspiration, 2019.
Photo: J. Anthony Martinez

PART TWO:
Workout Contributions

Introduction

You will remember that my advice in the middle of this book was to start slow to become fast. Remember not to do too much too soon. After all, if you are injured or over-trained, you cannot arrive at your superhero self. Even the great Kamehameha the Great knew this. In times of peace, he still prepared his warriors with vigorous training. Thus, when it was time for battle, they had months or even years of hard work that prepared them for running fast and being strong.

It would be best to learn proper sprint mechanics. The warm up includes some of these basic movements that emphasize full range of motion in the shoulder swing/arm movement as well as the snapping down of the leg so that the toe is dorsi-flexed and the foot strikes under your hip on the ball portion. Heel striking is like putting on the brakes and should be avoided. The "A" skip, the "B" skip and the "C" skip are all examples of these, although there is a current trend to leave out the "B" skip.

I asked experienced master's sprinters for some advice that they might pass along to the beginner sprinter. Here are a few of the pieces of advice from these folks who have experienced a return to sprinting or beginning to sprint:

Start gradual, stretch, and have fun!
—Max Garcia

Start slow and build up to a full training routine. Recovery is so important and becomes even more so the older we get. Log your sessions to include weather, diet, life stresses, workout results so you can assess what changes need to be made along the way.
—Rachel Guest

Create a long term foundation of strength training along with excellent sleep habits! For a beginner, I think strength training should ideally be done for a significant amount of time before heavy sprint training begins. AND regular massages!
—Bernice Bragg

Make sure your feet are working properly.
—Wilson Soo-Hoo

Expect it will take 6 months before you can be ferocious again. Do buildups over 75 meters- slow, medium, then fast.
—Dolf Berle

Lots of warming up and lots of sprint mechanic drills.
—Amanda Roberts

Weight lifting is critical. Work into it, work into the speed work, back off when you feel tight. Get feedback on form. Cool down completely, with mobility work.
—Ruth Janjic

Sprinting is a strength event. Start lifting and you'll get faster.
—Regina Flory

Start slow, take rest days, try not to do too much too soon. Try not to be too hard on yourself. Love what you do.
—Deneath Edwards

Do some tests to assess where you are right now. Design training with numbers based on that with some kind of gradual performance progression. A savvy wise coach sure can be helpful mostly to hold you back a little.
—Dave Albo

Get a training buddy and be sure to schedule rest days. Do not run when injured.
—Linda Carty

Start slow, weight train, rest, cross train and just have fun.
—Dennis Jones

Your past does not define you. No matter if you have been sedentary your whole adult life, today can be the beginning of something new and unique. It's worth a chance.
—Chris Holloman

Do ALL the burpees.
—Alexandra Jones

Focus on endurance and speed endurance because getting strong is easier than getting fast. Once you have good speed endurance, then incorporate speed workouts. Drink lots of water. This will reduce your chance of injury.
—Richard Hill

Try to remember what it felt like to let loose and run like a kid. Run a little, rest a little, run a little more. Don't stress.
—Cathy Palmer Nicoletti

Learn how to stretch and do it often.
—Mitch Lyster

Make sure your legs are strong enough to take the increased stress. Lots of leg exercises to build strength. I also like running/sprinting up a hill. Not too steep but enough to cause you to drive into the grade. Work on your form. Video is a great tool to see how you are actually doing.
—Ed Rose

Understand the dynamics of phases of the race and constantly work on proper techniques.
—AJ Mason

Commit to the process and embrace the journey. Optimal results show up in years 2-3.
—Durran Dunn aka Mr. Freeze

Another great source for support in beginning sprinting is USATF Masters Track at USATF.org The joy of seeing others being their superhero selves is inspiring to say the least. I have had a wonderful experience representing my country in international meets alongside my USATF "track family."

Photo: J. Anthony Martinez

Section I. Beginner Sprint Training

CONTRIBUTOR: Cynthia Monteleone
PURPOSE/GOAL: Priming the muscles gradually for eventual sprinting.
Instagram Fastover40
Twitter: Fastover40
MAM808.com
YouTube: MAM: Metabolic Analytics Maui Cynthia Monteleone

Hill Workout Once a Week:

Week 1-4: Find a hill and time yourself walking up it for approximately 2:45-3 minutes. Walk back down. Repeat until you are able to accomplish 10 hills.

Week 5-8: Begin to try to jog up the hill. Walk back down. Repeat until you are able to jog 10 hills.

Week 9-24: Begin to increase the pace of your hills. Try to run the last one as your fastest and time yourself. Attempt to beat the time from the week before. Walk back down as your rest period.

Advanced: Same as above but slowly shuffle jog back down for less rest.

Super Advanced: Same as above but slowly shuffle jog back down and alternate 50 crunches and 10 squat jumps between hills.

Field Workout (On Grass) 1-2 times a week, 10 reps

PURPOSE/GOAL: Beginning running workout on grass to provide soft surface for ease on shins and joints.

First Phase: Run for 8 seconds, walk back for rest.

Second Phase: Run for 10 seconds, walk back for rest.

Third Phase: Run for 8-10 seconds, increasing speed as the reps go, taking 3 minute break in between.

Section II. Short Sprint Training

Lion Martinez
Photo Courtesy of Lion Martinez

CONTRIBUTOR: *Master's World Champion Lion Martinez*
PURPOSE: *Short Sprinting (50m-100m training)*
Instagram: lionmartinez

Lion Martinez, M35 100m World Champ, M40 200m World Champ, M40 100/200m European Champion, has been coaching sprints since 1998. Lion is one of the best sources for information on sprinting. He is a successful athlete and coach because he has a broad knowledge base of what works.

This workout is designed to work short speed endurance by depleting the ATP/creatine levels in your muscles which forces the mitochondria to store and produce more energy from these sources, without having to tap into your glycogen storages and the following lactate production. Basically, it will allow you to produce more power longer which means you will slow down later.

This has been a staple workout for me and my athletes for over a decade and has thoroughly improved both my 100m and my 200m performance.

This is a highly intense session that will tax your central nervous system, so please be mindful of your fatigue and hydration at all times. Being properly warmed up is vital and I implore you to be well rested before attempting it (in other words, no eccentric leg training or sprints the day before).

Also be sure to work this in progression in a format you can handle, where you increase either intensity or volume week by week but never both. You are never supposed to go flat out but rather aim to maintain good form and posture.

The Workout:
Warm up dynamically including sprint drill and perhaps some light jumping exercises (use examples given in this book). Always perform the first set at a moderately lower pace to make sure the body is ready, never push it.

Week 1: Perform 2 sets of 3x50m sprints (or 60m if male, or advanced female), at 85% of maximum (calculate 50m or 60m max time/0.85).

Rest intervals include walk-back between reps, and a 2-minute rest between sets.

Week 2: As above but add a set (3x3x distance).

Week 3: As above but add a rep per set (3x4x distance).

After 3 weeks, depending on your programming (such as a rest week), restart the workout but go 90%. Each following 3 weeks, add about 2-3% of intensity. For each intensity level, increase rest:

90% = 1 min/3 mins (1 minute rep rest, 3 minute set rest)
92% = 2 min/4 mins
95% = 3 min/6 mins
98% = 3-4 mins/8 mins

When you can comfortably perform 3x4x60m at 98% you should be well conditioned and ready to do a decent 100m in competition. Again, please be very mindful of rest and recovery as well as workout prep, with all that it encompasses.

When you start to get more advanced after a couple of months, distance can be increased to 80m for a really tough workout but I truly suggest never completely moving away from the shorter distance, because a longer distance means working other energy systems and all are needed to be a good and complete sprinter.

Lion Martinez

My daughter, Sanya Richards-Ross and Ato Boldon at the Millrose Games 2019

Ato Boldon
Courtesy of Ato Boldon

CONTRIBUTOR: Ato Boldon
PURPOSE: Short Sprinting
Instagram: atoboldon

Ato Boldon is an NBC Sports Broadcast Analyst on Track and Field, Olympic Champion Sprinter, and 4-time Olympic medal winner from Trinidad and Tobago. He holds the national records in the 50, 60, and 200m. Ato is one of my absolute favorites and one the the all-time bests in the sport (in my humble opinion!) His knowledge of form and execution of sprinting is the best I've seen.

The Workout:
7x 100m starting at the 400m start line and walking/jogging back 50m.

Do 2 sets with 10 min rest in between sets.

CONTRIBUTOR: Dale Upton
PURPOSE: Short Sprinting
Instagram: dunamisathletics

For Canadian Speed Coach Dale Upton, coaching education is very important and he continues his certifications in high level coaching programs yearly. His philosophy is: "To provide a training atmosphere where athletes have peace of mind in knowing that no matter their ability level, they will reach a level of self-satisfaction in their athletic ability directed by themselves and the coach."

He is the owner and head coach of Dunamis Athletic Training which focuses on speed development and agility training for track and field, figure skating, hockey, soccer, and high school and university football athletes. He has produced multiple champion athletes. I met Coach Dale on Maui years ago when helped me develop a better warm-up that targeted dynamic movements. He is a treasure in his knowledge of sprint mechanics.

The Workout:

Anaerobic Power:

Run 40m at 90% effort capacity four times, resting 30 seconds to 1 minute between sprints. Repeat 2-3x with 3-5 minute rests between sets.

OR

Sprint, Float, Sprint (Sprint, Float, Sprint means to drive hard, then back off and float with good form, then drive hard again.) 10m/10m/10m with 40m acceleration at 95% with rest at 6-8 min.

Alactaid Capacity:

Run a 150m then 2 min rest. Then 4 x 40m with 2 min rest in between. Then one 150m all at 90%. Do two sets of this with a set rest of 6-8 min.

OR

Basic Speed Endurance:

Run 40m, 30m, 20m at 95% resting 30 seconds to 1 min between sprints. Repeat sequence 3-5 times with a 6 minute rest between sets.

CONTRIBUTOR: Maggie Malone
PURPOSE: Short Sprinting
Instagram: maggietheaggie

Maggie Malone, 2020. Photo: Josh Huskin

Maggie Malone is a Rio Olympian
for the Javelin. Maggie is my favorite
warrior princess. The Javelin reminds
me of the ways of the Ancient
Hawaiians, who often used sprinting
and spears in their training. Maggie is a
true champion in mind, body and spirit.

The Workout:
Sprint 50 yards
jog back rest.
Goal: see how many you can
do in 10 min.
Target: Men: 24 ;
Women: 20

Maggie and Me, 2020

Section III. Medium Sprint Training

CONTRIBUTOR:
Christa Bortignon
PURPOSE: *Medium Sprinting*
FaceBook: Christa Bortignon

Christa Bortignon is a World
Champion Masters Athlete Sprinter
and currently age 83 ½. She is a
multiple World Champion and
record holder in several events.
Christa always has a positive, work-
hard mentality. She strength trains a
few times a week. You can find my
interview with her on my youtube
channel (MAM: Metabolic Analytics
Maui Cynthia Monteleone). She shows
us that there are no excuses—sprinting
can be done at any age!

Christa, 2018. Photo: Dave Albo

The Workout:
Start out with 2-3 easy walks around the track.

The last one, alternate 50m walking, 50m light running. Then do 15
minutes of ABC sprint drills including 3 x 50m strides.

Start with 100m or 200m depending on how you feel. Then a few shorter ones
like 3 x 50m or 80m-60m-40m. Then finish off with another 100m or 200m.

*On some days after track training, she takes 10 discus throws, or 5 long
jumps and 5 triple jumps after digging the pit for 10 minutes. She finishes
with stretching.

*On days not at the track, she does strength training. She recommends Earl
Fee's book "100 Years Young the Natural Way" in which he recommends
strength training to combat loss of muscle as we age.

CONTRIBUTOR:
Rachel Guest
PURPOSE:
Medium Sprinting
Instagram: fsttrck

There isn't enough paper to list Rachel's accomplishments, but I'll give a quick summary: She has three American Records (not counting relays) in the Pentathlon and Heptathlon. She is a five time World Champion, the top world ranked short hurdler, high jumper, and combined events athlete. She has won Athlete of the Year five times. She also has over 40 National Championship titles. I love when I get to run on a relay with Rachel. No matter what, she puts her game face on and rises to the challenge. I admire her strong will to be a champion and her dedication in her execution to make it happen.

Rachel Guest
Photo Credit: Dave Albo

The Workout:

2 x 300m with 5 minute recovery

7 minute set rest

2 x 100m with walk back rest

Target times will vary depending on athlete/gender/skill level. This workout would be 6-12 weeks after you begin sprint training.

CONTRIBUTOR: Annie Kunz
PURPOSE: Medium Sprinting
Instagram: anniekunz7

Annie is a hard worker who is a
beautiful person inside and out!
She radiates positive energy and
is brilliant at her craft. She is a
national champion Heptathlete.
Multi-eventers are true warriors:
sprinting, jumping and throwing
their way to victory like the
Ancient Hawaiians.

The Workout:
Decreasing ladder

400m at 85-90% rest 5 minutes

300m at 85-90% rest 5 minutes

250m at 85-90% rest 6 minutes

200m at 85-90% rest 6 minutes

150m at 85-90%

Annie Kunz 2019 by Von Ware

Annie and me, 2020

CONTRIBUTOR: Durran Z Dunn, AKA "Mr. Freeze"
PURPOSE: Medium Sprinting
Instagram: Durranzrunner

Durran Dunn is a regional, nation, and world champion sprinter whose positive outlook leads him to be a success at everything he does.

The Workout:
TWO SETS OF: 250m/150m at 60% effort.

4 minute rest in between the 250/150 and 10 minute set rest

Gradually work up to 90 second rep rest and 8 minute set rest at 80-85% effort.

Photo courtesy of
Durran Dunn

CONTRIBUTOR: *Emma McGowan*
PURPOSE: *Medium Sprinting*
Instagram: emmamckog

Emma is a multiple World Champion Track Sprinter. In the World Championships in 2019, she completed the "Sprint Trifecta" winning all three of the sprints: the 60m, 200m and 400m at age 51. She is a kind and generous person with a tough, beast-mode champion persona on the track. She has been amazingly supportive of me and I absolutely adore her. Emma is a warrior that is worth watching and learning from!

The Workout:
100m run

100m jog

200m run

200m jog

300m run

100 jog

3 sets with a 400m walk in between sets

Photo:
Dave Albo

Section IV. Long Sprint Training

CONTRIBUTOR: Manteo Mitchell
PURPOSE: Medium Sprinting
Instagram: manteomitchell

Manteo Mitchell is an Olympic Champion, Silver Medalist. Manteo is such an inspirational individual. During his Olympic race, his leg broke halfway and he continued to keep running and qualified his relay team for the ultimate silver medal. His continuous strength and determination is a prime example of superhero mentality!

The Workout:
HILLS: 8 times 150M Hill; Jog back rest.

Cues: Nice, strong, even pace. Rest: Jog down halfway, walk the remaining back to the start of the hill.

TECHNICAL DAY: Complete warm-up routine and hurdle walks.

4 x each Sprint Drills

Manteo, Indoor 2020
Photo courtesy of Manteo Mitchell

4 x 15 seconds seated arm drill

4 x 50m acceleration strides

4 x frequency drill over cones

5 min rest between

20-30 MIN TECHNICAL WORK:
3 x 30m from fall start

3 x 30 m from 3 point start

3 x 30 m fly-ins, walk back rest

Manteo and me,
December 2019

2 x 20 m freeze jumps (squat and jump for distance, freeze on landing)

2 x 4 lunge jumps

2 x 20 m walking lunges, walk back rest

Phyllis Francis 2019.
Photo: Dave Albo

CONTRIBUTOR: *Phyllis Francis*
PURPOSE: *Medium Sprinting*
Instagram: Philly_phyl88

Phyllis Francis is an Olympian, World
Champion 400m Elite. Phyllis is my
favorite 400m sprinter! Her positive
attitude and hard work ethic is so
motivational and inspiring!

The Workout:
2 sets of: (5x 200m) at 85-90% with 3
minute rest in between each and 10
minute set rest

CONTRIBUTOR: Coach Rudy Huber
PURPOSE: Medium Sprinting
Facebook: Rudy Huber
RUNNERSPARADISE.COM

Coach Rudy Huber is my running
coach. I am extremely grateful for his
knowledge, patience, and motivation
during my quest to become a World
Champion.

Coach Huber is a local track and field coach and a running director
in Hawaii. He has resided in Hawaii since 1994 and has been a major
player in bringing in new and exciting running and extreme events to the
island. He has coached some of the best sprinters in the state from many
schools around the islands. He has been fortunate enough to coach both
high school and college athletes, as well as post college. He has a B.S. in
Physical Education, a M.S.S. in Sports Coaching and Marketing. He is a
Level 2 USATF certified coach specializing in the areas of sprinting. Coach
Huber was an All-American at Cal State Poly in San Luis Obispo, where
he competed in sprints, jumps and relays. In his career Coach Huber has
coached dozens of state track and field champions, as well as National and
World Champion athletes.

The Workout:
A WEEK OF WORKOUTS

Beginner 400 Meter Workout

"I have a lot of favorite workouts for beginners, who want to run the 400
meters and even the 200 meters. But before we even get to that point, I
make sure that the athletes are in reasonable condition, doing resistance
training, working on their core, and the like. You have to have a good base
in order to increase your work load and intensity. So being in reasonable
condition is important.

"So, after I feel that the athlete is in reasonable condition, I love doing the
following workout. This works on their speed endurance, tempo and form.

We want the athlete to be as consistent with their finish times and rest times as possible. If the athlete can do this workout a couple of times and hit their times consistently throughout the week, then we adjust rest or goal times. So, the coach must make realistic goals and rest times for the athlete to achieve. This will get the athlete stronger to handle more intensity later. I usually like to do this workout on a Monday. Start the week off with a BANG!!

"Here is the workout that I would give a beginning athlete and adjust if needed."

Monday: 8-10x 200m (85%)(3 minute rest)
Easy walk across the grass, back to the start. Concentrate on relaxed breathing for each interval and during rest time.
Also make sure arm swing is close to full range of motion and picking up hips.

Tuesday: Form drills, form running (accelerations 30-60 meters x 8), core work, cool down.

Wednesday: Light plyometrics day, add controlled 20-30 meters (85% accelerations) after each set of plyometric drill. Constantly moving, with very little rest.

Thursday: Pool workout day and concentrate on good movement, breathing and relaxation, core work

Friday: 1x600 (thru 400 @ 85-95%) (3 minute rest), 2x200(80%) (3 minute rest) x3

Weekend: Rest

Huber with me and my daughter, 2018

CONTRIBUTOR: Rose Green
PURPOSE: Medium Sprinting

Rose Green is a Multiple World Champion Masters Athlete Sprinter, currently age 83. Rose is a great example of training hard at any age. I met Rose at my very first track meet and we have been cheering each other on ever since. She strength trains and keeps consistent in her running training.

The Workout:
Train at Least 3 times each week with a mix of warm up (400m a couple of times) and drills to get the body prepared for the runs.

For the 400m you would do a series of 350m runs with 30 seconds rest; 200m, 150m and so on. Depending on your fitness level, you might have to make some adjustments. Strength training is a must. Stay hydrated and eat right to maintain strong muscles.

Rose coming out of the blocks. Photo: Dave Albo

Section V. Strength Training Programs

My best advice is to start reading and watching as much as possible from the legend, my mentor, Charles Poliquin. To say the man was a genius is an understatement. He likened strength training to learning a language. There are several levels to it and just like a language, the goal is to become as fluent as possible. He used to say you know you truly understood another language when you could make a joke in it.

Charles and me, 2018

My second piece of advice is to find strength coaches who have studied under Charles and hire them or learn from them. The strength coaches who contributed here are all top students of Charles and are thriving as coaches for amazing athletes from the high school level all the way to Olympian and professional athletes. Learning strength coaching techniques from Charles was one of the best experiences of my life. I now get to enjoy watching other athletes benefit from his wisdom passed down through me. Seeing an athlete I strength coached this year win the award for best female wrestler in the nation 2020 from USA Wrestling, was better than winning the gold medal myself. My passion is helping others. I hope these examples point the way to help you as well!

Here are some basic beginner strength training programs targeted toward developing the strength needed for sprinting. I love the use of tempo in strength training because it recruits more muscle fibers and decreases chance for injury because you are using a slow controlled movement with less weight.

If you have questions about what some of the exercises are or how to proceed, please feel to reach out to me at Mam808.com.

How to read tempo: For example in a squat: (3-1-1-0) would be read as follows: Eccentric movement (down) in 3 seconds, pause 1 at the bottom, come up in one second, no pause at the top. An "X" indicates to perform that movement as fast or explosively as possible.

A1 – indicates the first set of the "A" series. If there is an A1 and an A2, it indicates a superset. You would complete all sets of the A series before moving on to the B series.

Photo: Margaret Monteleone

CONTRIBUTOR: Preston Greene
PURPOSE: Strength Training

Photo courtesy of Preston Greene

Preston Greene of Florida Gators Basketball, was named a legend and one of the best strength coaches in the country by *ESPN* and S*ports Illustrated* in 2020. Level 5 International Certified Poliquin coach, in his 10th season with the Gators. I am so grateful to have Preston as a new mentor.

The Workout:
Beginner dumbbell (DB) workout 3 week cycle:

DAY ONE:
A1 - Heel elevated DB Squat (3-0-1-0) 4 x 10-12 Rest: 60s
A2 - One arm DB row (3-0-1-0) 4 x 10-12 Rest 60s
B1 - Back Extension (3-0-1-0) 3 x 10-12 Rest 60s
B2 - Flat DB Bench Press Neutral Grip (3-0-1-0) 3 x 10-12 Rest 60s
C1- Hammer Curl (3-0-1-0) 3 x 10-12 Rest 45s
C2 - Lying DB Tricep Extensions (3-0-1-0) 3 x 10-12 Rest 45s
C3 - Incline Garhammer Raise (2-0-1-1) 3 x 10-12 Rest 45s

DAY 2:
A1 - DB Lunge (3-0-X-0) 4 x 10-12 Rest: 60s
A2 - Incline DB Press (3-0-1-0) 4 x 10-12 Rest: 60s
B - 1 Lying Leg Curl (3-0-1-1) 3 x 8-10 Rest 60s
B2 - DB Lateral Raise (2-0-2-0) 3 x 10-12 Rest 60s
C1 - DB Overhead Triceps Extension (3-1-1-0) 3 x 10-12 Rest 45s
C2 - DB Calf Raise (2-2-2-2) 3x 10-12 Rest 45s
C3 - Front Plank (Tempo: Iso) 3 x 15s week 2: 3 x 20s week 3: 3 x 25s

DAY 3:
A1 - DB Step Up Mid –Shin height box (3-0-1-0) 4 x 10-12 Rest 60s
A2 - Bent Over DB Row (3-0-1-0)4 x 10-12 Rest 60s
B1 - DB Romanian Deadlift (3-1-1-1) 3 x 10-12 Rest 60s
B2 - Seated DB Shoulder Press (3-0-1-0) 3 x 10-12 Rest 60s
C1 - DB Supinated Curl (3-0-1-0) 3 x 10-12 Rest 45s
C2 - Push Up (3-0-10) 3 x 10-12 Rest 45s
C3 - Bench Crunch (2-0-1-1) 3 x 10-12 Rest 45s

CONTRIBUTOR: Malcolm Gwilliam
PURPOSE: Strength Training
SOURCEPERFORMANCE.COM

Malcolm Gwilliam of Source Performance is a Strength Coach to Olympians and Professional Athletes. Malcolm is my strength coach. His dedication to precision in writing individual strength programs is unmatched. He has helped to make me as strong of a warrior as I am today and for that I am extremely grateful!

Photo of Malcolm courtesy of SourcePerformance.com

"Results are delivered from incorporating years of experience working with world-class athletes." —Source Performance

The Workout:
Beginner Sprint Program

Phase 1 - Performed Twice Per Week for 3 Weeks

A1 Split Squat - Front Foot Elevated - Level 2 - DB - 4x8-10 - 4-1-X-0 tempo - 90 seconds rest

A2 Leg Curl - Kneeling - Foot In - Dorsiflexed - Unilateral - 4x 6-8 reps - 4-0-X-0 tempo - 90 seconds rest

B1 Step-Up - Heel Elevated - 30 Degrees - Level 1 - DB - 4x15,12,12,10 - 2-0-1-0 tempo - 60 seconds rest

B2 Back Extension - 45 Degrees - Front Loaded - DB - 4x 8-10 reps - 2-0-1-4 tempo - 60 seconds rest

C1 Calf Raise - Seated - 3 Positions - 3x15-20 reps - 1-1-1-1 tempo - 45 seconds rest

C2 Garhammer Raise - 15 Degree - 3xMAX reps - 2-0-1-0 tempo - 45 seconds rest

Phase 1 notes:

- The X denoted in the tempo prescription during the A series exercises is placed to reinforce the athlete to have maximal intent during the concentric (upwards) motion of the lift.
- Paused split squats strengthen the VMO and gluteus maximus in the lengthened position of knee flexion. The 1 second pause eliminates 25% of the elastic energy produced through the stretch shortening cycle requiring a greater recruitment of motor units within the muscle cells of the VMO and gluteus maximus to produce a more forceful muscle contraction.
- Unilateral kneeling leg curls recruit the muscle fibers of the hamstrings as knee flexors. The toe turned inward places more emphasis on the semi-membranosous of the hamstring complex which is typically the weakest, therefore reducing strength discrepancies and a higher risk of hamstring injury.

Malcolm and me, 2020

• Heel elevated step-ups strengthen the VMO in the shortened position at knee extension, which aids in reducing the stance phase, the point when both feet touch the ground when running.

• Back extensions should be a staple in any running program. The four 4 second accentuated isometric pause at the top position places the erector spinae muscles under stress resembling what they are exposed to in order to maintain a vertical running posture.

• Change your foot position every set on calf raises from in, neutral, out.

CONTRIBUTOR: *Jon McDowell*
PURPOSE: *Strength Training*
TRAIN-VIVE.COM
Instagram: Jmacfitness

Photo courtesy of Jon McDowell

Jon McDowell of VIVE Personal Training is a Texas native, and has been an elite personal trainer for over twelve years. He graduated from the University of Texas in Arlington. He is accredited through USAW, USATF LV1 as well as ISSA. In addition, he holds his Metabolic Analytics, Procession Nutrition, and Fascial Stretch Therapy Practitioner Certifications.

Currently, he is one of the only trainers in Dallas certified in CANS, YPSI, Metabolic Analytics, and Biosignature analysis. In 2016, Jon co-opened VIVE Personal Training gym. Not only does he implement a system that involves foundational movement and performance benchmarks but also accompanies it by a systematic and progressive method of measuring performance progress. Jon is one of my favorite students of Charles'. He is the go-to guy for sprint training.

The Workout:
BEGINNER PROGRAM FOCUS ON FORM AND EXECUTION
LOWER BODY I WORKOUT:
5 sets

A. DB Squat heels elevated (6-0-X-0 tempo)
-Pre fatigue method
20sec isometric
-followed immediately by 6-8 repetitions
-6sec lower
-Stand back up fast
-Rest 90sec then repeat 5 rounds
4 sets x 8-10 repetitions

B1. Front foot elevated DB split squat (3-2-1-0 tempo)
-3sec lower
-2 sec pause at bottom
-rest 75 seconds then start B2

B2. Hamstring curl (6-1-1-0 tempo)
If doing slide disk.

-start in glute bridge position
-lengthen legs slowly 6 seconds until straight
- fast return
-rest 75 seconds then go to back B1
-complete 4 rounds
3 sets x 10-12 repetitions

C1. Heel elevated DB step up (1-0-1-0 tempo)
Controlled up & down motion
Rest 30 seconds then go to C2

C2. Plank to leg extension
-4 second slow leg raise
-1secons contract at the top
-2 second lower
-rest 30 sec start back with C1
-complete 3 rounds

UPPER BODY I WORKOUT:
5 sets x 8-10 repetitions

A1. DB chest press from floor (Or Push up)
Advanced
-pre fatigue: 15-20 second isometric hold
Followed by 8-10 repetitions.
Or
Intermediate
4-0-X-0 tempo
4sec lower
Up fast

A2. Half kneeling Neutral grip pulldown (4-3-X-0 tempo)
-Pull Down fast
-3 sec hold with elbows back
-Return slowly for 4 seconds to start
-rest 90seconds then start A1

-complete 5 rounds total of A series
4 sets x 8-10 repetitions

B1. Overhead DB press (tempo 4-0-1-0)
-Press up fast
-Control the lowering of weight for 4 secs
-Rest 75 seconds then go to B2.

B2. Kneeling or push up position DB Row (tempo 3-1-1-0)
-Pull the weight to hip
-Pause 1 sec
-Return slowly for 3 sec to start in arc motion
-Rest 75 seconds start back with B1. -Complete four rounds total of B series
3sets x 10-12 repetitions

C1. Band Bicep curl (tempo 3-0-2-0)
-Curl up keeping tension for 2 sec
-Lower for 3 seconds keeping tension
-Rest 60 seconds then start C2.

C2. Dumbbell or Band tricep extension (tempo 3-1-1-0)
-Press up under control
-Lower for 3 seconds
-Rest 60 seconds then start C1
-Complete 3 rounds total of C series

More from VIVE online workouts.

CONTRIBUTOR: Ronnie Incerta
PURPOSE: Strength Training
OAKFIT.COM
Instagram: Oakfit

Ronnie Incerta is the owner and founder of OAKFIT, LLC and a strength & speed coach. He is a USA Weightlifting National Coach, USA Track & Field State Coach, Poliquin Level 5 International Coach, and Poliquin BioSignature Practitioner. Ronnie has shown time and again that he is one of the best strength coaches in the country. His success with every level of athlete and his winning personality show that he is a true warrior himself and champion trainer of superhero warriors!

The Workout:
Phase One (3 Weeks)

Day 1 - Total Body
A1. Depth Jump - Reactive - 8in Low Box x 3 x 10 @ X0X0 Rest 60 Seconds
A2. Plank - Arms Extended - Shoulder Taps x 3 x 20 total @ 1111 each Rest

60 Seconds

B1. Split Squat - Front Foot Elevated - Low Pulley/Cable x 3 x 10-12 @ 4010 Rest 60 Seconds
B2. Seated Cable Row to Chin - Rope x 3 x 15-20 @ 2010 Rest 60 Seconds

C1. Standing One Arm DB Press - Neutral x 3 x 10-12 @ 4010 Rest 60s
C2. Seated Good Morning - Barbell x 3 x 10-12 @ 3010 Rest 60s

Day 2 - Total Body

A1. Depth Jumps - Reactive - 8in Low Box x 3 x 10 @ X0X0 Rest 60 Seconds
A2. Plank - Arms Extended - Shoulder Taps x 3 x 20 total @ 1111 each Rest 60 Seconds

B1. Step Up - Below Knee Height x 3 x 12-15 @ 2010 Rest 60s
B2. Seated Cable Row - Neutral - Medium x 3 x 15-20 @ 2010 Rest 60 Seconds

C1. Flat DB Bench Press x 3 x 10-12 @ 4010 Rest 60 Seconds
C2. Prone Lying Hamstring Curl x 3 x 8-10 @ 3010 Rest Seconds

Phase 2 (3 Weeks)

Day 1 - Total Body

A. Squats - Barbell - Heels Elevated x 4 x 8 @ 4010 Rest 150 Seconds

B1. Incline Bench Press - Barbell x 4 x 8 @ 4010 Rest 60 Seconds
B2. One Arm DB Row - Supported - Kneeling on Bench x 4 x 10-12 @ 3010 Rest 90 Seconds

B1. Lunges - Alternating - In Place x 3 x 10-12 @ 2010 Rest 60 Seconds
B2. 45 Degree Back Extension x 3 x 12-15 @ 2010 Rest 60s

Day 2 - Total Body

A. Deadlift - Hex Bar x 4 x 6 @ 4010 Rest 150 Seconds

B1. Decline Bench Press - Dumbbell x 4 x 8-10 @ 3010 Rest 60 Seconds
B2. Seated Cable Lat Pulldown - Neutral x 4 x 10-12 @ 3010 Rest 90 Seconds

C1. Powell Raise - Side Lying on Bench x 3 x 10-12 @ 3010 Rest 60s
C2. Hip Extension with Hamstring/Leg Curl x 3 x 12-15 @ 3010 Rest 60s

Phase 3 (3 Weeks)

Day 1 - Total Body
A1. Depth Jump - Reactive - 12in Mid Box x 3 x 10 @ X0X0 Rest 60 Seconds
A2. Plank - Arms Extended - Shoulder Taps x 3 x 20 each @ 1111 Rest 60 Seconds

B1. Split Squat - Dumbbell x 3 x 15-20 @ 3010 Rest 60 Seconds
B2. Kneeling Hamstring Curl - Single Leg Only x 3 x @ 2010 Rest 60 Seconds

C1. Seated DB Press - Neutral Grip x 3 x 12-15 @ 3010 Rest 60s
C2. Seated Cable Row - Close Semi-Pronated Grip x 3 x 15-20 @ 2010 Rest 60s

D1. Horizontal Back Extension x 3 x 15-20 @ 2010 Rest 45s
D2. Low Ab Drill - Knees Bent x 3 x 15-20 @ 2010 Rest 45s

Day 2 - Total Body

A1. Depth Jumps - Reactive - 12in Mid Box x 3 x 10 Rest 60 Seconds
A2. Plank - Arms Extended - Shoulder Taps x 3 x 20 each Rest 60 Seconds

B1. Step Up - Above Knee Height x 3 x 15-20 @ 2010 Rest 60s

B2. Prone Lying Hamstring Curl x 3 x 8-10 @ 3010 Rest Seconds

C1. Flat DB Bench Press x 3 x 12-15 @ 3010 Rest 60 Seconds
C2. Seated Pulldown - Neutral - Medium x 3 x 15-20 @ 2010 Rest 60 Seconds

D1. Supine Ab/Lower Body Twist x 3 x 15-20 each side @ 2010 Rest 45 Seconds
D2. Push Ups* x 3 x 15-20 @ 2010 Rest 45 Seconds (* = on Incline/Box if necessary, not from knees)

Phase 4 (3 Weeks)

Day 1 - Total Body

A1. Squats - Barbell - Heels Elevated x 4 x 6 @ 3010 Rest 150 Seconds

B1. Incline Bench Press - Barbell x 4 x 6 @ 3010 Rest 60 Seconds
B2. One Arm DB Row - Supported - Kneeling on Bench x 4 x 10-12 @ 3010 Rest 90 Seconds

C1. Lunges - Alternating - Forward Moving x 3 x 15-20 each @ 2010 Rest 60 Seconds
C2. RDL - Dumbbell x 3 x 12-15 @ 2010 Rest 60s

Day 2 - Total Body

A1. Deadlift - Barbell - Rack Above Knee x 4 x 6 @ 32X0 Rest 15 Seconds
A2. Vertical Squat Jumps - Explosive/Reactive x 4 x 10 @ X0X0 Rest 150 Seconds

B1. Decline Bench Press - Dumbbell x 4 x 6 @ 2010 Rest 60 Seconds
B2. Seated Cable Row to Chin - Rope x 4 x 10-12 @ 2010 Rest 90 Seconds

CONTRIBUTOR: Cynthia Monteleone
PURPOSE: Plyometrics

(AKA WW Wednesday workout, video on youtube)
      a. 40 hops over line, 25 jumping jacks, 50 crunches x 3 sets
      b. 40 double leg hops over line,25 high knees, 100 bicycles x 3 sets
      c. 20 lunge jumps, 25 jumping jacks, 50 toe touches x 3 sets
      d. 20 tuck jumps, 25 high knees, 100 flutter kicks x 3 sets
      e. Bench toe touch x 60, 70, 80 touches with 10 seconds rest ea set
      f. 20 jump squats followed by 25 full leg raises
      g. 20 burpees followed by 50 6 in. leg raises
      f. Walking lunge x 200
      g. Advanced: Run 200, 50 crunches, run 200

Alternative Plyo Workout great for general conditioning:

Corner Warrior Workout (also available on YouTube):
Location: Football Field
Run from outside goal post to corner at full stride, not jogging. Perform first exercise. Run to each corner then stop and perform an exercise. Every 4 laps is a short water break.
At corners perform each of the following:

Lap
1 50 crunches at each corner (4 x per lap)
2: 100 bicycles at each corner
3. 50 toe touch at each corner
4.100 flutter kicks at each corner

Water 10 seconds
1. 50 shoulder walks
2. 15 push ups
3. 20 sun salutations
4. 15 Narrow push ups

Water 10 seconds
1. 20 squats
2. 20 split squat jumps
3. 10 squat jumps
4. 10 burpees

Photo: J. Anthony Martinez

Photo: J. Anthony Martinez

My Favorite Products

Charles Poliquin
Maui Cattle Company
Punakea Palms Coconut Farm
Shawn Baker: The Carnivore Diet
Dr. Sean O'mara
Dr. Gabrielle Lyon
Mike Mutzel/ Myoxience
ATP Labs
Source Performance
OAKFIT
VIVE Training –Jon McDowell
Dunamis Athletics, Coach Dale Upton
NutriDyn
Designs For Health
Saucony Running
Lululemon
Under Armour JRod Trained
Gill Athletics (Starting Blocks)
Writing Room ATL
J. Anthony Martinez Photography
Dave Albo of lane1photos
Margaret Monteleone Photography

Fast Over 40 Recipe Bible Cookbook coming soon!

Endnotes

1 Kawena, Mary Puku'i. *The Olelo No'eau: Hawaiian Proverbs and Poetical Sayings.* Bishop Museum Press: (March, 1983).

2 Kawena, Mary Puku'i. *The Olelo No'eau: Hawaiian Proverbs and Poetical Sayings.* Bishop Museum Press: (March, 1983). p. 281

3 Ellis, William. "Polynesian Researches," Fisher, Son and Jackson, Newgate Street, 1831. p.115

4 Kirchhoff, Phillipp, et al. "An Amino Acid Transporter Involved in Gastric Acid Secretion." *Pflügers Archiv: European Journal of Physiology* (March, 2006).

5 Cordiero, LMS et al. "Physical Exercise-Induced Fatigue: The Role of Serotonergic and Dopaminergic Systems." *Brazilian Journal of Medical and Biological Research* (October, 2017).

6 Dantzer, Heijnen et al. "The Neuroimmune Basis of Fatigue." *Trends in Neurosciences* (October, 2016).

7 Schuber, Mitchell L. "Gastric Secretion." Current Opinion in Gastroenterology (November, 2014).

8 Dallas, David C. et al. "Personalizing Protein Nourishment." *Critical Reviews in Food Science and Nutrition* (October, 2017).

9 MacArthur, Katherine, et al. "Soy Protein Meals Stimulate Less Gastric Acid Secretion and Gastrin Release than Beef Meals." *Gastroenterology* (October,1988).

10 Mohr, Alex, et al. "The Athletic Gut Microbiota," *Journal of the International Society of Sports Nutrition* (July, 2020).

11 Aroutcheva, A. et al. "Prevotella Bivia as a Source of Lipopolysaccaride in the Vagina." *Anaerobe* (November, 2008).

12 Monteleone. "Prevotella, Sprinting, Health and Happiness," mam808.com, (August 2020).

13 There are no other indications in the history books on which foods were defined as "soggy."

14 Malo, David. "Hawaiian Antiquities, Fornanders History of Ancient Hawaii." Bishop Museum Press, 1951. Chapter 44 notes.

15 Kolata, Gina. "Eat Less Meat Scientists Said, Now Some Believe That Was Bad Advice." *New York Times* (September, 2019).

16 Wolf, Robb. Diana Rodgers. *Sacred Cow*. BenBella Books, Inc. (July, 2020).

17 Berry, Ken interview with Lone Star Keto Girl (July, 2020).

18 Dallas, David C. et al. "Personalizing Protein Nourishment." *Critical Reviews in Food Science and Nutrition* (October, 2017).

19 Lambert, EV et al. "Nutritional Strategies from Promoting Fat Utilization and Delaying the Onset of Fatigue During Prolonged Exercise." *Journal of Sports Science* (June, 1997).
Hargreaves, Mark, et al. "Pre-Exercise Carbohydrate and Fat Ingestion: Effects on Metabolism and Performance." *Journal of Sports Science* (January, 2004).

20 Paoli, Antonio, et al. "Ketogenic Diet Does Not Affect Strength Performance in Elite Artistic Gymnasts." *Journal of International Sports Nutrition* (July, 2012).

21 Epple, Elissa. Elizabeth Blackburn. *The Telomere Effect*. Grand Central Publishing (January, 2017) pgs. 220-221.

22 Branch, Stacy Matthews. "Unexpected Relationship Between Red Meat Diet and PBMC Telomere Length."
Fretts, Amanda, et al."Processed Meat but Not Unprocessed Red Meat is Inversely Associated with Leukocyte Telomere Length in the Strong Heart Family Study." The Journal of Nutrition (October, 2016).

23 Maurya, Vaibhav, et al. "Factors Influencing the Absorption of Vitamin D and GIT: an Overview." *Journal of Food Science and Technology* (November, 2017).

24 Ellis, William. *Polynesian Researches*. Fisher, Son and Jackson, Newgate Street London, 1831*, Vol. 1.*

25 Lissak, Gadi. "Adverse Physiological Effects of Screen Time on Children and Adolescents." *Environmental Research* (July, 2018).

26 *Hawaii News Now Word of the Day*, Hawaiinewsnow.com video: Hawaiian word of the day: Olakino (August 16, 2019).

27 Ryan, Maggie. "Cardio Isn't the Best Way to Burn Belly Fat." Popsugar/ Msn.com online (May, 2019).

28 Correia, PR, et al. "Increased Basal Plasma Derived Neurotrophic Factor Levels in Sprint Runners." *Neuroscience Bulletin* (2011).
Heibsz, P. et al. "Changes in Exercise Capacity and Serum BDNF Following Long Term Sprint Interval Training in Well-Trained Cyclists." *Journal of Applied Physiology* (2019).

29 TheriChadorneshi, Hossein. "Comparing Sprint and Endurance Training on

Anxiety, Depression and Its Relation with Brain-Derived Neurotrophic Factor in Rats." *Behavioural Brain Research* (2017).

30 Heydari, M., Freund, J. et al. "The Effect of High Intensity Intermittent Exercise on Body Composition of Overweight Young Males." *J Obes* (June, 2012). Hutchinson, Alex, "Sprinting for Weight Loss: Are Catecholamines the Secret?" Runners' World (July, 2012).

31 Chaillou, Thomas. "Skeletal Muscle Fiber Type in Hypoxia: Adaptation to High Altitude Exposure and Under Conditions of Pathological Hypoxia." *Frontiers in Physiology* (2018).

32 There are multiple studies on EMF (Electromagnetic Frequency) and RF (Radio Frequency) and its harmful health impacts. Some include but are not limited to: Deruelle, Fabien. "The Different Sources of Electromagnetic Fields: Dangers are not Limited to Physical Health." *Electromagnetic Biology and Medicine* (2020). Belyav, Igor, et al. "Europea[m] EMF Guideline for Prevention, Diagnosis and Treatment of EMF-Related Health Problems and Illnesses." *Reviews on Environmental Health* (2016). Di Ciaula, Agostino. "Towards 5g Communication Systems: Are There Health Implications?" *International Journal of Hygiene and Environmental Health* (2018). Bortikiewicz, Alicja. "Health Effects of Radiofrequency Electromagnetic Fields." *Ind Health* (2019). Miah, Tayaba, et al, "Current Understanding of the Health Effects of Electromagnetic Fields." *Pediatric Annals* (2017). Sage, Cindy, et al. "Electromagnetic Fields, Pulsed Radiofrequency Radiation, and Epigentics: How Wireless Technologies May Affect Childhood Development." *Journal of Child Development* (May, 2017). Wall, Stephen, et al. "Real-World Cell Phone Radiofrequency Electromagnetic Field Exposures." *Environmental Research* (2019).

33 Koziorowksa, Anna, et al. "Extremely Low-Frequency Electromagnetic Field (EMF) Generates Alterations in the Synthesis and Secretion of Oestradiol-17beta in Uterine Tissues." *Theriongenology* (2018). Kiray, Amac, et al, "The Effects of Exposure to Electromagnetic Field on Rat Myocardium." *Toxicology and Industrial Health* (2013).

34 Please see drgabriellelyon.com for an extensive list of articles and protocols

35 Walker, Matthew. "Why We Sleep." Scrinber (2017).

36 Kraemer, William. "The Effects of Soy and Whey Protein Supplementation on Acute Hormonal Responses to Resistance Exercise in Men." Am Coll Ntr (2013). Impey, Samuel, et al. "Whey Protein Augments Leucinemia and Postexercise p70sk1 Activity Compared with a Hydrolyzed Collagen Blend When in Recovery from Training with Low Carbohydrate Availability." *International Journal of Sport Nutrition and Exercise Metabolism* (November, 2018).

Morifuji, Masashi, et al, "Dietary Whey Protein Increases Liver and Skeletal Muscle Glycogen Levels in Exercise Rats." *Journal of Nutrition* (2005).

37 Ter Host, Kasper, et al. "Fructose Consumption, Lipogenisis, and Non-Alcoholic Fatty liver Disease." *Nutrients* (2017).

38 Bobel, Till S, et al. "Less Immune Activation Following Social Stress in Rural vs. Urban Participants Raised with ..." *Proceedings of the National Academy of Sciences of the United States of America* (2018).
Johnson, Arthur, "The Hygiene Hypothesis." *IEE Pulse* (2016).
Berstad, AE. "Does Reduced Microbial Exposure Contribute to Increased Prevalence of Allergy?" Tidsskr NOr Laegeforen (2000).

39 Meyer, Stephanie. "Environmental Xenoestrogens Super-Activate a Variant Murine ER Beta in Cholagiocytes." *Toxicological Sciences* (2017).
Marino, Maria. "Xenoestrogens Challenge 17b Estradiol Protective Effects in Colon Cancer." *World Journal of Gastrointestinal Oncology* (2014).
Wozinak, Milena, et al. "Xenoestrogens: Endocrine Disrupting Compounds." *Ginekologia Polska* (2008).

40 Rosado, Phillipe. "Marine Probiotics: Increasing Coral Resistance to Bleaching through Microbiome Manipulation." *The ISME Journal* (2019).

Acknowledgments

I would like to acknowledge my Ohana (family) who have helped me create this guide, including my parents who are always wonderful, supportive and loving, my husband who lifts me up, providing my solid foundation and encourages me to be exactly who I am, and my kids for their love and inspiration. Thank you to my local community and my friends for always being there for me, my coaches Rudy Huber and Malcolm Gwilliam for pushing me to do my best with their precisely crafted coaching. I am so grateful for my contributors for taking the time to share their high levels of knowledge to help teach us all how to be Superheroes. Thanks to my editor for being ultra amazing, easy to work with and a beautiful person. This book would not be the same without the work of my favorite photographers, Dave Albo, J. Anthony Martinez and Margaret Monteleone for capturing the essence of the moment in perfect artistic form. Last, but certainly not least at all, my current mentor Preston Greene who stepped in to answer all of my crazy questions after we lost Charles. His patience and passion for helping me continue to spread the wisdom Charles taught us is greatly appreciated.

About the Author & Illustrator

CM (Cynthia) Monteleone is a certified Metabolic Analytics Practitioner whose clients range from Olympians and professional athletes to patients her doctor sends to her for consultation. She has a passion for helping others achieve health and happiness by finding their ultimate superhero self. She is a wife, a mother of three, a multiple National Champion and a World Champion. You can connect with CM on Instagram or Twitter @fastover40 or on her website at MAM808.com. You can also visit her YouTube channel at MAM Metabolic Analytics of Maui for fresh content and videos relating to this book.

Printed in Great Britain
by Amazon